WHAT THE F.R.E.D!

MASTERING THE FOUR ESSENTIAL TRAITS FOR AN UNSTOPPABLE MINDSET

BY FREDERICK A. MARTINEZ

WHAT THE F.R.E.D!

MASTERING THE FOUR ESSENTIAL TRAITS FOR AN UNSTOPPABLE MINDSET

BY FREDERICK A. MARTINEZ

Published by:
Frederick Martinez, Optimal High Performance Strategist
Website: fredmartinez.info
Website: wtfredbook.com
Facebook: https://www.facebook.com/whatthefredbook
Instagram: https://www.instagram.com/wtfredbook/

Paperback ISBN: 978-1-962570-04-6
EBook ISBN: 978-1-962570-05-3
Audiobook ISBN: 978-1-962570-07-7
Ingram Spark ISBN: 978-1-962570-06-0
Library of Congress Control Number:2023917767

TABLE OF CONTENTS

TRAIT #1: F = FOCUS

TRAIT #2: R = RESILIENCE

TRAIT #3: E = ENERGETIC

TRAIT #4: D = DRIVEN

UNSTOPPABLE MINDSET

APPENDIX

Acknowledgments

I am eternally grateful to the people who taught me the true meaning of unconditional love: my mother, Ramona Martinez; my father, Alejandro "Alex" Martinez II; my brothers, Alex Martinez III and Leroy Martinez; my sisters, Yvonne Diaz, Karen Martinez, and Sharon Martinez. Their love and guidance have been instrumental in shaping who I am today. I am forever in their debt for the sacrifices they made and the endless love they have given me throughout my life. I cannot thank them enough for their profound impact on me and for showing me what true love looks like.

I am deeply grateful to my childhood friends, who played such a significant role in shaping my life. Your presence in my life made my childhood an unforgettable journey of fun and excitement. I will always cherish the memories we shared, big and small, and I am forever grateful for your impact on me. Without our shared experiences, I would not be who I am today. Thank you from the bottom of my heart.

I am deeply grateful to the coaches and mentors who have played a vital role in my journey. Their guidance and encouragement have helped me become who I am today. I am so thankful for the time and effort they invested in me, pushing me to be better than I was yesterday and helping me to reach my full potential. I will always be grateful for the knowledge, skills, and wisdom they have imparted. Their impact on my life has been immeasurable, and I will always carry their teachings with me. Thank you with heartfelt gratitude.

Lastly, I want to express my deepest gratitude to my teammates. Your unwavering support and camaraderie have been a constant source of inspiration and motivation for me. Your encouragement and push to greatness have helped me to achieve more than I ever thought possible. I am honored to have had the opportunity to work and grow alongside such an amazing group of people. I will always treasure the memories and experiences we shared. Thank you for being my teammates and friends and helping me become the best version of myself.

Introduction

I want to share with you a fundamental truth that can transform your life. Are you ready for it? Here it is: 80% of success is in the mindset. That's right - your thoughts, beliefs, and attitudes play a crucial role in determining whether you achieve your goals and live a life of true fulfillment.

You see, success isn't a matter of luck or chance. It's a matter of mindset and a willingness to take action. The good news is that you can cultivate a winning mindset that empowers you to overcome any obstacle and achieve greatness in all areas of your life.

The first step is to evaluate your current mindset. Do you believe in your ability to succeed? Do you have a growth-oriented attitude that embraces challenges and opportunities? If not, it's time to start working on your mindset.

Research shows that your thoughts and beliefs have a significant impact on your ability to achieve your goals. That's why it's essential to cultivate an optimistic and growth-oriented mindset that enables you to overcome obstacles and seize opportunities.

To develop an unstoppable mindset, you need to master the four pillars of focus, resilience, energy, and drive. These qualities are the foundation of success, and with dedication and perseverance, you can master them.

Focus is about maintaining a laser-like concentration on your goals and priorities. Resilience is about bouncing back from setbacks and adversity. Energy is about having the physical and mental stamina to pursue your goals relentlessly. And drive is about channeling your passion and ambition into action.

When you develop these four qualities, you become unstoppable. You have the power to achieve your wildest dreams and live a life of success and fulfillment.

So, my friends, I urge you to start working on your mindset today. Invest in yourself and commit to developing the qualities that make an unstoppable mindset. You deserve to become the best version of yourself and live the life you've always dreamed of.

The world is waiting for your greatness, and with an unstoppable mindset, you can achieve anything you set your mind to. So, let's get to work and unleash our true potential!

WTF (WHAT THE F.R.E.D)

Maintaining a focused, resilient, energetic, and driven (F.R.E.D) mindset demands a unique approach in a world filled with constant distractions and unavoidable challenges. These traits are not innate; rather, they are developed through experience, education, and determination. In my journey, I have discovered that the key to success lies in cultivating an unstoppable mindset that can weather any storm.

F.R.E.D, is a system I created based on my life story. F.R.E.D stands for "Focused, Resilient, Energetic, and Driven," It embodies the principles and practices that have helped me overcome obstacles and achieve my goals. Through F.R.E.D, I hope to share my experiences and insights with others looking to develop their unstoppable mindset.

You will find my background that drove me to seek change and find my best self. As you continue to read, you will discover the philosophy behind F.R.E.D. and its potential benefits for those who embrace it. Whether you are a student, an entrepreneur, an athlete, or simply someone looking to improve your life, F.R.E.D can help you unlock your full potential and achieve your desired success. So, let's dive into the world of F.R.E.D and discover how to be focused, resilient, and energetically driven, no matter what life throws your way.

During a Dale Carnegie leadership training class, a fellow participant commented on my story about overcoming obstacles. He remarked that I was like the Phoenix; I had emerged from the ashes, forged by fire, and had become stronger than ever before. This compliment left me beaming with happiness, and I did not realize I had impacted someone because I did not know my worth then.

Before taking this training class, I felt like discarded trash because of the story I was telling myself.

Let me share my journey of transformation that led to my unstoppable mindset. It's important to remember that every individual's journey is unique, and their experiences and challenges will vary. I am sharing my story to encourage you that we can overcome difficult times in our lives. Despite the differences in our struggles, we can all strive to overcome them and come out stronger on the other side.

Personal Story

Hello everyone. I am Frederick Martinez; my friends call me Fred, Freddie, whatever you call me. Just don't call me late for dinner. I am honored you are reading my book. I want to talk about something that affects all of us at some point in our lives: feeling not good enough, experiencing rejection, feeling worthless, not fitting in, struggling with perfectionism, fearing failure, having unrealistic expectations, comparing ourselves to others, and experiencing trauma. These are all heavy topics, but I want to share some powerful life lessons and examples that can help you overcome these challenges.

My story will talk about some life challenges that plague us all at some point in our lives. It's the feeling that we're not good enough, the fear of rejection, the belief that we're worthless, the idea that we don't fit in, the trap of perfectionism, the fear of failure, the weight of unrealistic expectations, and the never-ending cycle of comparison.

It's easy to get stuck in these negative thought patterns, especially in a world where we're constantly comparing ourselves to others on social media. We see their highlight reels, and it's easy to forget that we're only seeing a small part of their lives. We forget that everyone has struggles, failures, and setbacks.

The truth is that your value is not based on your accomplishments or failures, your position in life, the size of your bank account, or even how many people have liked your most recent post. You must acknowledge and accept the innate value you possess. It took me four decades to get to this conclusion, and I'm still working through it.

As a child, I struggled with a learning disability that made school incredibly difficult. I was often told that I would never amount to anything, that I was not good enough, and that I would never fit in. When I played sports, I was the last one picked; I was often overlooked because of my height. But I refused to let those negative opinions and voices define me. I worked harder than anyone else and eventually graduated with an electrical engineering degree and represented the United States in International Weightlifting competitions. That was the first time I proved to myself that I was capable of achieving anything I set my mind to.

First, let's talk about not feeling good enough. For a long time, I struggled with feeling like I wasn't good enough for anything. I felt like I wasn't smart enough, talented enough, tall enough, or even attractive enough. But then I realized that these thoughts were holding me back from achieving my full potential. I had to change my mindset and start believing in myself. I had to realize that I am good enough and that I have something valuable to offer the world.

I remember when I was in high school, I tried out for the sophomore basketball team. I was so excited at the prospect of finally fitting in and being part of a team. But after a grueling week of tryouts, I was cut from the team. I felt like a failure. I felt like I wasn't good enough. And worst of all, two weeks later, I went to the coach's office to have a conversation with him because I heard a couple of students became ineligible to play because of grades. I asked if I could be part of the team because there were some openings now. He told me I was too short to play on his team.

But you know what? Looking back on it now, I realize that getting cut from the basketball team was one of the best things that ever happened to me. Because it taught me a valuable lesson: that rejection is not the end of the world. In fact, rejection is often the catalyst for something better. I used that rejection as fuel and focused on running track; I eventually became a college division one track sprinter years later at New Mexico State University.

You see, when we're rejected; it's easy to feel like we're not good enough. But the truth is rejection is not a reflection of our worth as a person. It's simply a sign that we need to keep pushing forward and striving for something better.

However, life had more challenges in store for me. My marriage of 15 years hit a rough patch, and it was a devastating blow. I longed for intimacy and affection from my wife, but she seemed to shut me down every time I tried to reach out to her. Even a simple hug was met with resistance, as she would push me away, causing me to feel unwanted and unloved.

I tried to do everything I could to show her my love and commitment, from cooking breakfast and dinner to leaving love notes and sending flowers. However, it seemed like my every action was misunderstood, and she believed I had some ulterior motive behind it.

The constant rejection and misinterpretation of my actions left me feeling emotionally drained and empty. The person I had shared so many beautiful moments with suddenly felt like a stranger to me. The love and connection we once had seemed to have vanished, leaving me with an overwhelming sense of loss and heartbreak.

Despite my efforts to save our relationship, it felt like my attempts were futile, and we were drifting apart. The loneliness and pain of feeling rejected by someone I loved so deeply were almost unbearable.

But through it all, I held onto hope that things would improve and that the love we once shared could be reignited. I refused to give up on our relationship and continued to work on it, even during the toughest moments. We had an upcoming road trip and thought it could be a time for us to reconnect.

The memory of that terrifying moment still sends shivers down my spine. We were two hours into a five-hour road trip to attend her sister's college graduation and celebrate her success in becoming an Air Force officer, and everything was going smoothly until it wasn't.

As we drove down the highway, a massive semi-truck suddenly veered into our lane, causing us to swerve dangerously close to the edge of the road. In a split second, we were faced with a decision: either collide with the merging road sign or risk being sideswiped by the truck.

The fear that gripped me at that moment was overwhelming. I felt helpless, watching as the truck barreled towards us and unsure of whether we would make it out alive. Every fiber of my being was consumed with the desire to protect my wife and ensure her safety; however, I wasn't driving, and I was not in control.

The sound of screeching tires and crunching metal still echoes in my ears, and the memory of the impact still lingers in my mind. The sheer force of the collision left us both dazed and confused, and it was a miracle that we were able to walk away with only minor injuries, and the car had minor damage.

Her anger was palpable, and I could feel the tension in the air. She was furious with me for not being behind the wheel, and her rage was only exacerbated by the careless actions of the semi-truck driver. At that moment, she was consumed by a desire for vengeance, a need to chase after the perpetrator and make him pay for his recklessness.

But I knew that giving in to her anger would only make things worse. So, I gently tried to reason with her, to calm her down, and to help her see reason. Yet, my efforts only seemed to add fuel to the fire. The last thing I wanted to do was to make things worse, and I soon realized that I had made a mistake.

As if things couldn't get any worse, we soon discovered that our radiator was busted, and our car was leaking coolant. It was clear that we weren't going anywhere anytime soon, and the realization only added to the frustration and anger we were both feeling.

At that moment, I felt lost and helpless. I wanted to do something, anything, to make the situation better, but I was at a loss for what to do. All I could do was sit there and watch as my wife's anger boiled over, knowing that there was nothing I could say or do to make things right. We had a near-death experience that left us stranded in a small town and possibly missing her sisters' ceremonies.

We called the DPS (Department of Public Safety) to report the incident and get a tow truck driver. The driver took us to a local mechanic, and his base operation was in a junkyard. When I walked into one of the buildings and couldn't see a soul, I got a weird and eerie feeling. I told the tow truck driver to take us to another mechanic, and he took us to an auto body shop. The owner was eager to work on the car, but I only needed him to fix it mechanically. He told me he had to do everything, but I reminded him that's not what I wanted. I only wanted the mechanical operations fixed, not the bodywork. Dealing with him and my wife, who was yelling at me to fix the car, was getting me very agitated.

As the situation unfolded, I could feel my anger and frustration mounting. The tow truck driver informed me that my insurance wouldn't cover another tow and I would have to pay for it myself. I immediately called the insurance company to try and work something out; at the same time, my wife was yelling at me, trying to pull the phone away from me because she wanted to be in control. I was able to convince the insurance company to approve another tow to a bigger town where they had a larger reasonable car repair shop and a car rental place.

At the car repair shop, I was communicating with the insurance company to cover the cost of the mechanical repair, and the bodywork would be done in our hometown, as we would be using the deductible. While I was on the phone, my wife had to take the phone away from me because the conversation wasn't going the way my wife had anticipated. I started feeling minimized and unappreciated, and I started to bottle up my emotions.

All the while, the stress of the situation was taking its toll on me. I didn't feel like a man, and I was angry with my wife for projecting her anger onto me. I could feel myself on the verge of exploding. Suddenly, without thinking, I ran in front of oncoming traffic. I wanted her to feel the pain of my loss. The cars slammed on their brakes, and the drivers yelled at me that they could have hit me. I screamed back, "You should have fucking hit me!" and ran for what felt like hours to release all the pent-up energy.

Looking back on the experience, I realize that it taught me an important lesson and one that I've carried with me ever since. I needed to communicate better instead of bottling up my emotions until they exploded, even when things were tough. Running away from your problems or lashing out in anger only causes more harm. I learned that taking a break or finding a way to release my emotions in a healthy manner is a better way to cope with stress. Most importantly, managing and controlling your emotions is the key to living a happy, stress-free life instead of letting out the savage beast of the incredible Hulk that resides in all of us. In the end, we got the car fixed, but I also gained some valuable insights about how to deal with difficult situations in a more constructive way.

Two months later, my world was shattered when I discovered that my wife had fallen in love with another person. In the face of this devastating revelation, I was told by both my wife and a marriage counselor that I needed to leave our home and stay with a friend. As I gathered my belongings and prepared to leave my home, I stumbled upon my gun. In a moment of despair and hopelessness, I placed the gun to my head, ready to end my suffering. I desired for her to comprehend the depth of my heartache and the fact that she was responsible for causing it. I wanted her to carry this pain with her for the remainder of her life. But at that moment, a sudden change occurred within me, and I couldn't quite explain what it was. Was it a divine intervention? I can't say for sure, but regardless, I found myself unable to follow through with pulling the trigger. I realized that my death would not solve anything, and I decided to use that moment to kill my old self and become a catalyst for change. I put down the gun, and I embarked on a journey of self-discovery and personal development.

This event marked a pivotal moment in my life and changed everything….

I developed a strong interest in self-improvement and made a commitment to surpass my physical and mental boundaries. By immersing myself in personal development and adopting stoicism, I focused on improving my emotional, mental, and spiritual wellness. I actively pursued guidance from specialists in hypnotherapy, relationship communication, life coaching, men's coaching, and mental toughness.

In one of my therapy sessions, I came to the realization that I had childhood trauma that I had minimized and never addressed. While it may not seem significant to some, the experience had a profound impact on me as a young child, triggering the fight-or-flight response in my brain. The trauma involved a nonsexual, non-consensual touch that occurred during a time when I was naive and sheltered in a strict household that didn't show much physical affection. This experience caused a deep sense of discomfort and unease that persisted into my adulthood, manifested in my reluctance to hug others unless I felt completely comfortable. Additionally, I found myself overcompensating to prove my worth, likely stemming from a lack of self-assurance resulting from the trauma. My therapist helped me recognize and confront the impact of this childhood trauma on my life, like regulating my emotions, building trust within myself instead of looking at others for approval, building a secure attachment style, and building a stronger self-image, higher self-esteem, and self-acceptance.

As we started to go deeper into the abyss to unpack the trauma that I used for fuel, you can only use so much of that negative energy as fuel until it has no impact on you whatsoever. I had one coach tell me, "You first do it for God, your Country, and then yourself." I wasn't even doing it for any of those things. I was doing it to prove to others that I was worthy.

One memory I had was when I was playing little league baseball during a game, my coach told me I couldn't hit the ball worth a damn and asked me to bunt. I said to myself I am going to show him I can hit the ball. On the first two pitches, I swung with all my might and missed. The coach was getting pissed off at that time, yelling from the dugout. On the third pitch, I tried to bunt, but it was a foul, which resulted in a strike. The coach was furious and took my bat, throwing it against the fence, calling me a loser, and benching me for the rest of the game.

Throughout my athletic career, I fed off the negative energy and abuse to push harder and harder to keep trying, taking those punches because I was relentless. Even though I can take the abuse, my mind does not know the difference and starts to believe the negative thoughts and words that I spoke to myself and others to me. The therapist did a timeline therapy on me going back to that specific time and changing the past in my mind. Timeline therapy is a powerful process and technique for personal change and growth by removing any painful, emotionally attached memories that are not serving you.

Which resulted in my not using the negative energy as fuel anymore to show others I am better than they are. Instead, focusing on myself and the outcome I want to achieve and compete against who I was yesterday.

I changed the way I competed in competitions. I did not view my opponents as the competition; I viewed them as my comrades together; we pushed each other to bring out the best version of ourselves that day. I stopped using the negative trauma to fuel my drive. I started focusing on what I wanted, always looking at the positive and reframing the negative into something positive. I started to have fun in my competitions; instead of playing mind games against my opponents, I was rooting for them to push themselves harder. With this change in mindset, I broke numerous records because I was not in my head anymore analyzing what I should do; next, I was just letting my performance show the results.

Looking back, I am filled with a sense of empowerment and inspiration. I am no longer the rejected kid, desperate for recognition and approval. I have transformed into a resilient fighter, an audacious dreamer, and a triumphant winner - despite any naysayers.

Working with a professional therapist to heal the broken pieces of your life can be a powerful and transformative experience. In order to rebuild a solid foundation, it's necessary to revisit past memories and create a database in your mind of all the obstacles you've overcome. This allows you to draw from that database for positive reinforcement when faced with setbacks, instead of falling into a negative spiral. By harnessing the power of your past struggles, you can find inspiration and strength to keep moving forward toward a brighter future.

In my last semester in college, I suffered a devastating knee injury while playing basketball that knocked me off my feet. Suddenly, everything became a daunting task, including attending classes, as I lived five miles away from the college campus and drove a manual car. For six months, I relied on crutches, and even getting around campus was an uphill battle. The injury took a toll on my academics, and it seemed like I might not graduate that semester. But giving up was never an option for me.

With the help of the dean of engineering, I found a way to remain a full-time student for insurance purposes, but getting to and from class remained a challenge. Despite the obstacles, I never lost hope. I remained determined to graduate, no matter what. I had to rely on the kindness of others for rides and even had to bribe them with the use of my car and handicapped parking.

However, setbacks are just temporary obstacles that can be overcome with grit and determination. After a long and arduous road to recovery, I was able to walk again and even drive. I finally achieved my goal, of graduating college a semester later. This experience taught me that if you truly desire something, you will find a way to make it happen.

I learned the importance of asking for help and never giving up on my dreams, no matter how difficult the road may seem. This experience not only taught me perseverance and determination but also inspired me to pursue my goals with even greater passion and enthusiasm.

My story is a testament to the power of perseverance, and I hope that it inspires others to never give up on their dreams, no matter how insurmountable the challenges may seem. I believe that by persevering and never giving up, we can overcome any obstacle and achieve greatness. So let us all remember to embrace challenges, learn from our setbacks, and never give up on our dreams, for they are within reach.

As I work with a counselor to examine the breakdown in my marriage, I'm faced with the difficult task of looking inward to identify the root cause. It's become clear that a lack of respect was at the heart of the issue, with many contributing factors. Through this process of introspection, I've come to the realization that my own lack of integrity played a significant role in the demise of my relationship. I failed to keep my commitments to my spouse and neglected to prioritize their needs. Instead of focusing on how I could make life easier for my partner, I was too preoccupied with my own challenges, such as the loss of my business. I recognize now that I failed to be a leader and take charge of the situations that needed to be handled. With the guidance of my counselor, I'm committed to learning from these mistakes and developing strategies to avoid repeating them in future relationships.

In my journey towards personal growth and becoming a stronger man, one of my counselors suggested that I participate in events with Sacred Sons. This organization provides a unique opportunity for men to heal and connect with other like-minded individuals on a journey toward transformation. Sacred Sons offer experiences designed to help men heal from past traumas and create a new model of masculinity grounded in love, connection, and purpose. Through their work, Sacred Sons aim to build a global community of men dedicated to self-discovery, emotional healing, and spiritual awakening. I find their mission to be truly empowering and inspiring, and I'm grateful for the opportunity to be a part of this incredible movement.

At the Sacred Sons event, I had the privilege to share my life journey with a group of men. Though I am not a father and at the age of fifty, I am too old to have a child because we will both be in diapers; I chose to tell my story anyway. As I recounted the past, it felt like it happened only yesterday - the time when I was 32 and learned that I would be a dad for the first time. It was a momentous occasion, filled with a mix of excitement and fear, and little did I know that it was just the beginning of a life-changing journey that would test my resolve and resilience.

Despite the initial elation, fate dealt us a crushing blow. We experienced a devastating loss when our son's brain did not develop and we had to go through the birthing process after the first trimester. As devout Catholics, we wanted to provide our child with the last rites, but many priests were hesitant to do so, mistakenly assuming that we were seeking an abortion. We induced labor to spare our son further suffering, and it was only with the help of a Franciscan Friar that we found solace and comfort during our darkest hour. Holding our lifeless child in my arms was a moment of pro-found sadness and grief, and it felt as though my dream of becoming a father was forever lost.

Undeterred, we persevered and tried to conceive again. But it wasn't easy - we struggled with fertility issues and eventually sought the help of an IVF specialist. Though the journey was filled with setbacks, I never gave up hope. Still, there were moments when I blamed myself, God, and the world for the challenges we faced.

To my surprise, the men at the Sacred Sons event didn't see me as a failure but rather as a wise and inspiring father figure. Their words of en-couragement and support touched my heart, and I realized that my story had the power to inspire and uplift others, even without biological children of my own. It was a transformative moment that gave me a renewed sense of purpose and a deeper appreciation for the impact I can have on the lives of those around me.

In our daily lives, we often take time for granted, assuming that we have an endless supply of it. However, time is a finite resource that is con-stantly passing, and we cannot slow it down or stop it. We may have a long list of things we want to accomplish, but time has a way of slipping away from us, leaving us wondering where it all went.

As the old saying goes, time waits for no one. It's important to recog-nize the fleeting nature of time and to make the most of every moment we have. By doing so, we can achieve our goals, enjoy our experiences, and live our lives to the fullest. In this context, the insight of Tim Grover that we can't manage time, but we can manage our focus becomes even more important.

It was a difficult experience watching both of my parents take their last breaths. They both expressed a strong desire for more time with their loved ones before passing away. Witnessing my mother's death was not as surprising to me as my father's. When he was diagnosed with pancreatic cancer, it was a shock.

My father was diagnosed with pancreatic cancer. One week he was doing yard work, and the next week he was bedridden. He was the one per-son I went to when I needed advice. He was my superhero. He was wise, ethical and he led by example. One important financial concept he taught me very early in my life was, "It's not how much you earn, but how much you save." He also had lots of creative ideas for saving money, like replac-ing the TV channel knob with an extra oven knob he already owned. As a child, my father taught me the importance of respect, such as making eye contact when shaking hands, offering a seat to a woman or elderly person, and walking on the outside of the street when with a significant other. He taught me to be open and humble. To not be afraid to ask for help, and most importantly, to understand that there are always three sides to a story - one's own perspective, the other person's perspective, and the truth. I miss him. My Father – My Superhero!

His sudden death was a shock to my family and me. He was diagnosed with pancreatic cancer and given just six months to live, but he passed away just six days later. This experience made me realize that I had taken my father's love and guidance for granted. I never had the chance to apologize for the trouble I caused him and my mother during my childhood and teenage years.

One memory I have was as a young and mischievous child; I once found myself in trouble and took the opportunity to make a break for freedom. I bolted out the door and sprinted down the block with my dad hot on my heels, brandishing his trusty belt. In my sarcastic way, I hollered back, "You'll never catch me!" But my dad was quick to respond, "Oh, you'll have to come home sometime, kiddo!" As a teenager, I once found myself facing off against my dad. I stood my ground, ready to throw a punch. But my father's response was calm and collected. With his unwavering energy and demeanor, he was able to defuse my anger and diffuse the situation.

Despite my occasional mischievous antics, my dad always maintained his composure and created a safe space for me to let off steam and cool down. With his level-headedness, he was able to handle even the most rebellious of behaviors.

It wasn't until years after my father's death that I truly understood the significance of his calm and collected approach. I had been so focused on running away from my emotions that I never fully processed them. In the aftermath of his passing, I tried to channel my pain into physical training, without any regard for the consequences. My reckless behavior eventually led to me tearing my rotator cuff during a weightlifting competition. It was a harsh reminder that, in my attempt to avoid dealing with my emotions, I was only causing more harm to myself. It was then that I realized the value of my father's approach and the importance of taking the time to process and work through our emotions.

Looking back, I now recognize the gift of witnessing my parent's last moments grasping for their last breath, as it has taught me to embrace my emotions and strive to become a stronger person. A stronger man is one who possesses physical strength, mental fortitude, emotional resilience, and a clear sense of purpose. It requires overcoming challenges, continuously improving oneself, and being responsible and dependable with strong moral values. Most importantly, I learned that time is precious and to cherish the moments with loved ones and not live with regret. Life is short, and we should strive to create memories and experiences that will bring us joy and fulfillment. It is also crucial that we do not allow ourselves to dwell on the past and instead, focus on living in the present moment and making the best of it. By embracing this mindset, we can avoid living with regret and be content knowing that we made the most of our time with those who matter most to us.

Through all of these challenges, I have learned some powerful lessons that I want to share with you today:

Lesson 1: You are capable of more than you think. You are not defined by your circumstances, your failures, or your struggles. You have the power to overcome anything you face and achieve your dreams.

Lesson 2: Failure is not the end. It's an opportunity to learn and grow. It's just feedback, embrace it, learn from it, and use it to become better.

Lesson 3: Comparison is another trap that can keep us stuck. We look at other people's lives and achievements and feel inadequate. But the comparison is a thief of joy. You are on your own journey, and you can't compare yourself to anyone else. Focus on your own goals, your own progress, and your own growth.

Lesson 4: Perfectionism is a trap that can hold us back. Don't wait for everything to be perfect before you take action. Just start, and adjust as you go. Focusing on progress, not perfection. Celebrate the small wins, learn from your mistakes, and keep moving forward.

Lesson 5: You are not alone. We all face struggles and challenges, but we also have the power to overcome them. Reach out for help when you need it, and don't be afraid to share your story.

Lesson 6: When dealing with a loss, open up your heart to give and receive love. I learned this the hard way when I lost my son to a brain defect after the first trimester. Instead of hiding and running away from the pain, to open up my heart to be there for my wife at the time. To love on each other to grow together from the loss instead of growing separately apart from each other.

Lesson 7: Learning to recognize and manage our own emotions, as well as empathizing with other people's emotions, can help build stronger relationships in the future.

Lesson 8: Open, honest communication opens the doors to building stronger relationships

Lesson 9: Prioritize self-care, dealing with difficult situations can be emotionally draining, and it's essential to take care of ourselves during this time. Prioritizing self-care, such as getting enough sleep, exercise, and therapy, can help move on and heal from experience.

Lesson 10: Don't rush into a new relationship: It can be tempting to jump into a new relationship after a breakup, but it's important to take time to heal and reflect on what went wrong in the previous relationship. Rushing into a new relationship can lead to repeating the same mistakes.

Lesson 11: The importance of vulnerability. It can be scary to open up and share your struggles with others, but it is also incredibly empowering. When we allow ourselves to be vulnerable, we create space for others to do the same. We build connections and community, and we break down the walls that keep us isolated and alone.

Lesson 12: Embrace rejection and use it as fuel to work harder, be more persistent, and develop a stronger mindset. Rejection is a natural part of the process of achieving greatness. All successful people view rejection as an opportunity to learn and grow rather than a setback or failure.

Lesson 13: Embrace your vulnerability. It is not a weakness but a strength. And through vulnerability, we can find the support and healing that we need to live our best lives.

Lesson 14: Embrace your individual uniqueness, your quirks, your strengths, and your weakness by stopping caring what everybody else thinks. Those traits make you who you are, and it's what makes you great.

Lesson 15: Realizing the Value of Time: A Lesson Learned When I watched my parents take their last breaths on their death beds was a sobering experience. It made me acutely aware of the preciousness of time and how easily we can take it for granted.

    As I sat by their side, I couldn't help but reflect on all the times I had wasted, all the moments I had let slip by without truly appreciating their value. It dawned on me that time is not a limitless resource, and once it's gone, it's gone forever.

The experience taught me to make the most of the time I have, to prioritize the things that truly matter, and to let go of trivial distractions. I learned to be more present in the moment, to savor the simple pleasures of life, and to appreciate the people I love.

Now, I strive to make each moment count, to use my time wisely, and to make a positive impact on the world around me. I have come to realize that time is our most valuable asset, and we should treat it with the utmost care and respect.

Lesson 16: If you or someone you know is experiencing suicidal thoughts, seek help from a healthcare provider immediately

Lesson 17: We all experience fear, but it's how we respond to fear that matters. Too often, we let fear hold us back. We're afraid of failure, of rejection, of not being good enough. But fear can be a powerful motivator. Use fear as fuel. Use it to push yourself beyond your limits to achieve things you never thought possible.

Thank you for allowing me to share my story. I'm so grateful even if you took a moment to read any part of it.

Until next time, remember that you are loved. You are not alone. You don't have to carry fear, anger, guilt, or shame. It takes courage and absolute vulnerability, but you can share your story, and you can experience deep healing — I did.

I want to leave you with these quotes that have always inspired me - "You were born an original, don't die a copy." Embrace who you are, be true to yourself, and don't let anyone tell you that you're not good enough. "Strength does not come from winning. Your struggles develop your strengths. When you go through hardships and decide not to surrender, that is strength." Remember, you are strong, capable, and enough, just as you are.

Discovering Myself

I came to understand the transformative power of affirmations in the form of "I am" statements during my own personal journey of self-growth. I was able to change my perspective and enhance my general well-being by deliberately selecting positive statements and repeating them to myself on a regular basis.

My mental processes and beliefs were rewired thanks to affirmations, which in turn changed how I felt and behaved. For instance, whenever I would get rejected, I would tell myself that I wasn't good enough. This rejection led to the myth that I was discarded trash and that no one desired me. I started to reframe this narrative and my critical self-talk by turning it into an uplifting affirmation that reflects my value and worth.

Here are some of the affirmations I used:

"I am valuable and worthy of love and respect."

"I am deserving of happiness and success."

"I am a unique and valuable person with strengths and talents to share with the world."

"I am confident in myself and my abilities, and I can overcome any challenge."

I've been able to stop negative self-talk and develop a more upbeat and confident self-image by making positive "I am" affirmations my go-to mantras. By focusing on the present and becoming more aware of my thoughts and feelings, these affirmations have improved my self-worth and confidence.

It's crucial to keep in mind that the things we say to ourselves have a big impact on how we feel. We may consciously build a positive self-image and an upbeat outlook on life by adding positive affirmations following "I am." This will make us happier and more fulfilled.

Affirmations are an effective tool for enhancing oneself and undergoing personal change when used consistently. They have the power to alter our internal conversations and bring about favorable adjustments in our life.

I have experienced firsthand the effectiveness of affirmations in creating an optimistic and empowering mindset that has enabled me to overcome challenges and attain my goals. I urge everyone to start using affirmations in their regular activities so they can see the difference they may have. If you have confidence in yourself, you can achieve everything you put your mind to.

When I look back on my life, I can see how my pain and mess have been the driving force behind my message to the world. I went through some difficult times (like losing my job, losing my house, holding my dead son in the palm of my hand, and loss of marriage) and made some not-so-great decisions (like running into oncoming traffic and putting a gun to my head), but what I learned from those experiences has been invaluable.

That's why I've embraced my acronym as a way to share my story with others.

My name is F.R.E.D. It stands for "Focus, Resilient, Energetic, Driven." I believe that our experiences form the basis for the stories we tell, both to ourselves and to others. When we're able to use our experiences to shape our stories, we're able to share our unique perspectives and make a real impact on the world.

What I've come to understand is that our pain and mess can actually be our message. We can use our stories to inspire, encourage, and heal. We can use our stories to help others understand and empathize with our experiences.

My acronym is a way of reminding myself that my experience can be my message. It's a reminder that my experiences are valuable and that my story can help others. It's a way of showing the world that our pain and mess can be turned into something positive.

So, if you're struggling with your own pain and mess, I encourage you to use it as an opportunity to create your own story and share it with the world. Your experiences are unique and powerful and can help to create real change.

Your pain and mess can be your message. Embrace it and share it with the world.

Growing up, I hated my name. I was constantly teased for it, with names like "Freddie Spaghetti," "Freddie Fender Bender," and "Drop Dead Fred." It felt like every other kid had a cool name, like my sports heroes Michael Jordan, Isaiah Thomas, or Magic Johnson, and I just wanted to fit in.

It wasn't until after college that I started to appreciate and embrace my name. I kept Fred as my casual name while going by Frederick professionally as an engineer. What I didn't realize at the time was that life has a funny way of working out.

As I grew older, I embraced my name and learned that it made me stand out in a crowd. I also found that my name was one of the oldest names, with its roots in Germanic languages and Anglo-Saxon. It means "peaceful ruler," and it was often given to a king who was wise and just.

I also realized that there were some famous people who shared my name, like Frederick the Great, who was a great strategist and was known for his military successes; Fred Astaire, the famous dancer, and Frederick Douglass, the abolitionist and a key leader in the fight for civil rights.

It turns out that there was something special about my name after all. I was never just "Freddie Spaghetti" or "Drop Dead Fred" - I was a Fred, a Frederick, and a leader. I learned to take my name and be proud of it and of all the incredible people who had come before me.

Life is funny, and sometimes it takes us a while to realize why we are the way we are. I'm glad I finally embraced my name, and all it stands for.

Having an understanding of the F.R.E.D traits is one thing, but applying them in our daily lives to develop an unstoppable mindset is another. Let's explore how to put these traits into action and make them a part of our daily routine.

How to Apply F.R.E.D to Your Life

An unstoppable mindset goes beyond just aspiration. It is a way of life and a continuing adventure. It's a mental condition of perseverance, focus, and clarity that allows someone to work hard to accomplish their goals. It is a way of thinking that empowers people to successfully meet every obstacle by producing positive results via effort and dedication.

Individuals with an unstoppable mindset accept responsibility for their actions rather than placing blame on others, and they are dedicated to their own personal development, which propels them to success.

To be successful, it's important to cultivate the right combination of focus, resiliency, energy, and drive. Focus helps us keep our eye on the prize and maintain our momentum toward success. Resilience allows us to bounce back from difficult experiences and stay focused on our goals, even in the face of adversity. Energy keeps us motivated and driven towards self-improvement so that we can push ourselves further than ever before. Finally, being driven means setting ambitious goals for ourselves and pursuing them with passion and determination until they're achieved. With these four components working together, anyone can achieve a true unstoppable mindset and become the best version of themselves.

It's not easy to master yourself, but it's worth the effort. With the right combination of Focus, Resiliency, Energy, and Drive, you can accomplish anything you commit yourself to. Take small steps each day towards reaching your goals, and use these four key elements as your guide. Remember that an unstoppable mindset is a journey and not a destination – enjoy every step of it! With consistency and dedication, you can achieve the unstoppable mindset you desire.

Celebrate your small victories along the way; they're just as significant. Don't forget to reward yourself for all of your hard work, and remember to celebrate each step forward that gets you closer to your goals. You deserve it. And don't be afraid of failure or setbacks; rather, take them as learning opportunities to become even more resilient in the pursuit of your goals. If you commit to it and remain focused each day, having an unstoppable mindset is a goal that is very doable. You can do this! Have trust in yourself and take action to achieve success.

After talking about What the F.R.E.D, let's get into the significance of focus.

TRAIT #1: F = FOCUS

When you focus on being a blessing, God makes sure that you are always blessed in abundance.¨Joel Osteen

What is Focus?

Focus, or the singularity of purpose, is one of the critical ideas for success in the modern world. Focusing all of our concentration on one goal will help us build the momentum needed to see our plans through to completion. Today's world is full of distractions, which makes it difficult to concentrate. But if we focus on a single goal, we may be able to ignore these distractions and achieve the desired outcomes.

Focusing enables us to direct our energy and apply all of our creativity to one task at a time. By doing so, we can focus more attention and energy on a single goal than if we try to accomplish too many things at once. Also, concentrating on a single goal gives us the satisfaction that comes from giving something our best, increasing the possibility that it will be achieved. Despite overwhelming odds against them, many people have succeeded in their chosen fields by using focus as their compass.

My Personal Story About Being Focused

Now that we have a good knowledge of what focus is. I will tell my own personal story on how having a focused mindset has impacted my life. The secret to realizing your potential and fulfilling your dreams is a focus. It allows you to focus your energy and attention on what is actually essential and to persevere in the face of difficulties. It empowers you to set clear goals and take consistent, purposeful action to achieve them.

We all have aspirations and dreams when we are young. We visualize ourselves making that last-second shot at winning the game, hitting a home run, catching a pass for a touchdown, and winning a race. If we can accomplish these things, then our peers will finally accept us. But as we age, we learn to understand that genuine approval and validation must come from within. And the key to achieving this is to focus on our goals and to persist through challenges and setbacks. It's not about proving ourselves to others but about pushing ourselves to be the best version of ourselves.

I want to share with you my own journey of discovery, of finding my true passion in life. It took me 20 years of competing in various sports before I finally discovered weightlifting. And I want to tell you that sometimes in life, we have to go through a journey of discovery to find our true passion and ourselves.

When I played sports as a child, I was often the underdog, overlooked for my talent because of my size. I remember the opposing team's cheerleaders would often say, "Oh, look how cute; he's so small." I always felt the need to prove myself, to show that I belonged. But after a while, that gets old because you're focusing on others and what they think of you instead of focusing on yourself and using that as the primary drive to be better than you were yesterday.

When I first started competing in the sport of Olympic lifting, my goal was to make it to the Olympic team trials. When you set a goal like that, you're focusing on shooting for the Moon. And just like President Kennedy said, "We choose to go to the Moon not because it's easy, but because it's hard." This statement has always resonated with me because it reminds me that if we're not reaching for the impossible, we're just existing. And if we're just living, what's the point?

The journey to making the Olympic team trials was not easy; it was full of obstacles, injuries, and challenges. But it was also full of growth, learning, self-discovery, and refocus. I want to remind you today that the journey to your dreams may be difficult, but it is worth it. So, let us all strive to shoot for the Moon and reach for the stars, not because it's easy, but because it's hard and it's worth it.

During my journey of self-discovery and self-development, I learned to let go of the need to prove to others that I belonged. I stopped competing and instead focused on enjoying the process and encouraging others to push themselves to their full potential. I realized that in life, we're not competing against others but against ourselves. If I'm not giving my best, I'm not only doing a disservice to myself but also to others who have the potential to push themselves further. This realization helped me to focus on my own progress and growth and let go of the need to compare myself to others. Remember, true success is not about proving yourself to others; it's about pushing yourself to be the best version of yourself.

I wish I could tell you a fairy tale ending to my story of making the Olympic team trials, but that's not how life works. I may not have landed on the Moon, but I did shoot for the stars. And through that journey, I broke and set numerous records, represented the United States in international competitions in my age group, trained at the Olympic training center multiple times, met countless individuals who were constantly pushing themselves to do and be better and had amazing coaches who became my mentors and even a second father to me.

It is important to remember that the journey itself is what matters, not the final destination. The lessons I learned along the way, the people I met, and the experiences I had all of it made me the person I am today. So, I urge you to take the time to discover your passion and shoot for the stars. Even if you don't land on the Moon, the journey itself will be worth it. Most importantly, when you focus on your goals and persist through challenges and setbacks, you will unlock your full potential and become the best version of yourself.

Now let us dive deeper into the specific strategies for harnessing the power to transform your life.

Unleash the Power of Focus to Transform Your Life

Are you ready to tap into the power of focus and transform your life? If you're seeking to achieve your goals faster and make the most out of every day, you've come to the right place. As Tony Robbins famously said, "Where focus goes, energy flows."

But don't just take it from me; let's hear it from Tim Grover, the renowned sports performance coach who has trained legendary athletes like Michael Jordan and Kobe Bryant. In his book *Relentless: From Good To Great to Unstoppable*, Grover emphasizes the importance of managing focus over managing time.

Why? Because managing your time alone won't necessarily lead to productivity or goal attainment. Instead, when you master the art of managing your focus, you're able to direct your energy and attention toward the most critical tasks that will move the needle toward your desired outcomes.

However, maintaining focus can be challenging without a clear vision and purpose. When faced with numerous inputs from different sources, it becomes difficult to direct your efforts effectively. To combat this, discipline is crucial in rejecting tasks that will not be executed, allowing you to concentrate on the one thing that will be done correctly and seen through to completion. Ultimately, the key is to focus on one outcome.

To focus on what matters most, it is essential to prioritize tasks that fall within your subject matter expertise (SME), which typically accounts for about 5% of your workload. Outsourcing the remaining 95% to someone with the appropriate expertise in that field can be more efficient and cost-effective, allowing you to maximize ROI (return on investment).

For instance, a former colleague of mine delegated his landscaping maintenance work to a professional, which allowed him to focus on his subject matter expertise as a software engineer. In exchange for the work done on his property, he agreed to operate and maintain the landscaper's website. This arrangement not only saved him time and effort but also allowed him to work in the comfort of his air-conditioned house while the landscaper benefited from having a professional website.

To determine your own subject matter expertise, you can use a simple approach inspired by Benjamin Franklin. List tasks that fall under "SME" (your expertise) on one side of a paper and "delegate" on the other. Delegating tasks that are not within your expertise can free up valuable time and energy for the tasks that matter most.

When delegating tasks, it is important to communicate your expectations and deadlines clearly and remain open to feedback and suggestions from the person assigned the task. This open communication can ensure that the task is completed efficiently and effectively and foster a sense of collaboration and mutual respect.

To achieve effective focus, it's essential to concentrate on what you want rather than what you think you need. Your focus should be crystal clear and captivating, drawing you toward it rather than having to push yourself toward it. Start by identifying where you currently are and where you want to be. Make your vision so compelling that you wake up with a burning desire to transform that area of your life. Reframe your thinking from "I have to do this" to "I get to do this," which will energize and drive you to take action and get things done.

Create a plan to provide guidance and enlist the help of a coach to hold you accountable. Look for someone who has experience in your desired area of expertise, as they can offer shortcuts and help you recalculate when necessary. Think of this person as your own personal GPS, similar to how we use GPS to navigate unfamiliar territory or avoid traffic delays. Why reinvent the wheel when someone has already achieved success in your chosen field? By following their lead, you can save time and money while getting closer to your goal at a faster pace. For instance, when I aimed to represent the United States in an international weightlifting competition, I sought out coaches who had trained Olympians. Now, I have no excuse for not turning my dream into a reality, and I can begin with proven strategies rather than trial and error.

If you have set your target and are receiving guidance from a mentor but are still not making progress toward your goal, it may be due to unresolved inner conflicts. In fact, 80% of success is attributed to mindset, while only 20% is based on skillsets and mechanics. Inner conflicts arise when your thoughts and actions are not aligned, resulting in a "one step forward, two steps back" situation akin to dancing. Some of these conflicts may stem from limiting beliefs, such as feeling undeserving of success despite having the necessary tools and talents. To move forward, you must first address these conflicts by asking yourself what truly matters to you rather than conforming to external pressures or past conditioning. Otherwise, you may achieve success, but it may not lead to fulfillment. Aligning your life with your values will create a clear path, allowing your habits to become standards and taking action without second-guessing yourself. In this way, you won't need to aim for the target as it will already be pulling you towards it.

To be successful in achieving your goals, it is essential to commit yourself to them while in an empowering state, or else you will not follow through. You have the power to control what you focus on by giving it more empowering meaning and following the actions of successful individuals. However, controlling your state is not an overnight process. It is a gradual progression that starts with developing rituals. Our rituals control us, as evident in people who maintain a healthy lifestyle by following a ritual of eating well and exercising daily. They have made it a habit and something they do regularly, such as walking instead of lounging on the couch or working out in the gym. These activities are uncomfortable for most people, but they continue to do them because they know they will yield results. Rituals can either put you in a positive state or take you out of it. For instance, distractions like social media, texting, and phone calls are rituals that take you out of focus and disrupt your state.

Getting yourself into an empowering state can be accomplished through various methods, including exercise, visualization, gratitude, positive affirmations, learning new things, and adjusting your posture. An effective technique that can be used anywhere is the Superman pose, which involves standing straight with your chest out and both hands on your hips. Research has shown that performing this pose for just two minutes before a significant event or challenging task can boost your testosterone levels and lower your cortisol levels, also known as your "take action" hormone. This increase in hormone levels can encourage assertive behavior and risk-taking while limiting self-doubt.

Whatever we choose to focus on has a tremendous impact on our lives. It has the power to determine whether we thrive in life or merely survive.

If you're constantly fixated on what's gone or what's lacking in your life, you're only setting yourself up for a vicious cycle of negativity. And trust me, that kind of pattern will only lead to frustration, depression, and stress. Do you really want to feel drained and defeated all the time? Of course not!

That's why I'm urging you to shift your mindset and focus on what you can control. Let's take action toward our goals instead of dwelling on the past or what's lacking. It's time to break free from the negative and start focusing on gratitude and appreciation.

Here's the thing, my friends. I firmly believe that we get what we focus on. If we choose to focus on negative energy, we'll only attract more negativity into our lives. It just reinforces what we don't want. But if we choose to focus on the positive, we'll attract more positivity into our lives. It's as simple as that.

So, let's make a choice to focus on the good. Let's take control of our thoughts and shift our focus toward what we want to achieve. I promise you this shift in mindset will change your life for the better.

If there's a story in your life that's holding you back, it's time to change that damn story. Don't use it as an excuse anymore; instead, use it to empower and uplift yourself. Let that story be the spark that drives you to transform your life for the better.

And if you're not yet living the life you want, it's time to cut the bullshit excuses. Stop telling yourself a story that you can't have what you want because of this or that. That's just a load of crap. The real reason you haven't achieved what you want is that you haven't fully committed yourself to burning the boats and to go all-in on your dreams.

Let me tell you, my friends, most of us give ourselves a way out, which is why we don't have what we want. But I've learned that true success comes when we have no other option but to see ourselves succeed, even if it means we have to die trying.

So, it's time to make a choice. Are you going to keep telling yourself the same old story, or are you going to take action and create a new story? The choice is yours, but I'm telling you, the world needs you to step up and become the best version of yourself. It's time to burn those damn boats and go all in on your dreams.

Listen up because I've got some game-changing advice for you. If you're looking to succeed and achieve your goals, then pay close attention. The truth is, everything you need to succeed is right in front of you - you just need to create a killer strategy, follow it with a laser-like focus, and adapt as needed.

Now, let me break it down for you. One of the most important strategies you can implement is starting and ending your day with a focus on your tasks. And I've got just the routine to help you do it.

But let me be clear - this routine is not a one-size-fits-all solution. You need to tailor it to your individual needs and preferences. Whether you're someone who pushes through work at lightning speed or someone who paces themselves with breaks and self-care, the key is to find what works for you.

Personally, I'm always refining my morning routine to optimize my mindset and productivity. I take advice from my mentors and adjust as needed to ensure that I'm starting my day off on the right foot.

Here are some habits that I recommend incorporating into your morning routine to help you cultivate focus and productivity:

First things first, start by consciously putting yourself in a positive frame of mind. Express gratitude for the opportunity to face a new day and make a difference. Ask for guidance and open yourself up to new possibilities.

Next, align your mind and body to work together harmoniously. This sets you up for success and helps you tackle your tasks with focus and determination.

So, there you have it, my friend - a simple but effective routine to help you start and end your day with a focus on your goals. Remember, if you don't finish everything you planned for the day, don't stress. Just resume it the next day and keep pushing forward. With the right strategy and mindset, you can achieve anything you desire.

Morning Routine

Note: Put your phone in airplane mode to limit distractions during your morning routine, such as checking emails or social media, to help cultivate focus and mental clarity. Save these activities for later in the day when your energy and focus are less likely to be depleted.

1. The first step to achieving success is to start your day with intention and purpose. That means waking up early every morning and setting aside time to plan your day and set your goals. But that's not enough. You must also make it a habit to make your bed first thing in the morning, setting a standard of excellence and achieving your first victory of the day. It may seem like a small task, but it's an important one. Remember, success starts with the little things. So, let's get after it and make today a great day!

2. Next drink 16 oz of water first thing in the morning can offer several benefits for your overall health and well-being. Adequate hydration is essential for optimal brain and body function, especially after a night's rest. Drinking water on an empty stomach can also help stimulate your metabolism, promote healthy digestion, and eliminate toxins from your body. As a result, you may experience more energy, support healthy weight management, and avoid digestive issues. By prioritizing hydration and making it a habit to start your day with a refreshing glass of water, you can set yourself up for a productive and energized day.

3. One way to start your day with a bang is by combining the benefits of red-light therapy, positive motivation, and meditation. Set aside 20 minutes in the morning to expose yourself to red light therapy while simultaneously listening to an inspiring audiobook or meditating to clear your mind. This practice can help you focus and concentrate better throughout the day, as well as uplift your mood and reduce stress levels. By incorporating this into your daily routine, you're not only improving your physical health but also nourishing your mental wellbeing. Additionally, by utilizing this time efficiently, you're making the most of your morning routine and boosting pro-

ductivity by achieving more in less time. So, make it a habit to prioritize this "no extra time" (NET) routine to start your day with a rejuvenated mind and body.

4. Physical activity has the power to elevate your emotional state and set your mind up for optimal focus. Whether you choose to pump iron in the gym, stretch your limbs in a yoga session or simply take a brisk walk in the great outdoors. When you engage in exercise, your body releases endorphins that help you feel energized, motivated and ready to tackle any challenge that comes your way. So why not make physical activity a non-negotiable part of your daily routine, and watch as your productivity and overall wellbeing soar to new heights? Remember, success is a result of consistent action, and there's no better way to set yourself up for success than by taking care of your body and mind through physical activity.

5. If you hit the sauna for 20 minutes after a workout, it can offer a range of benefits such as improving blood flow, reducing inflammation, enhancing cardiovascular function, boosting the production of growth hormone, and promoting better mental health. Additionally, since the muscles are already warm, stretching in the sauna can be advantageous. Nonetheless, it is crucial to seek advice from a healthcare provider before beginning a sauna regimen, especially if you have any pre-existing medical conditions.

6. Drinking electrolytes after the sauna is important because sweating during the sauna session can lead to dehydration and loss of essential minerals from the body. Electrolytes, such as sodium, potassium, magnesium, and calcium, help to maintain fluid balance in the body, support nerve and muscle function, and regulate heart rhythm. Replenishing electrolytes after a sauna session can help to restore the balance of these essential minerals in the body and prevent dehydration.

Moreover, the sauna can also cause a significant loss of sodium, which is an important electrolyte, through sweat. Sodium is crucial for maintaining proper blood pressure, nerve and muscle function, and fluid balance in the body. Therefore, consuming electrolyte-rich beverages or foods, such as coconut water, sports drinks, or bananas, can help to replace lost sodium and other electrolytes after a sauna session.

It is important to note that drinking electrolyte-rich beverages should not be a replacement for drinking plain water, which is essential for hydration. It is recommended to drink water before, during, and after a sauna session to prevent dehydration.

7. Eating a nutritional breakfast can help to improve focus and concentration throughout the day. When we wake up in the morning, our bodies are in a state of fasting, and the brain's glucose levels may be low. Glucose is the primary source of energy for the brain, and without enough glucose, our mental functioning, including focus and attention, can be impaired.

Eating a nutritious breakfast that includes complex carbohydrates, protein, and healthy fats can provide the brain with the necessary fuel to function optimally. Complex carbohydrates, such as whole-grain bread and oatmeal, release glucose slowly and steadily into the bloodstream, providing a sustained source of energy for the brain. Protein-rich foods, such as eggs or yogurt, can also help to improve focus by increasing the production of neurotransmitters, such as dopamine and norepinephrine, which are essential for attention and focus.

Furthermore, eating a nutritious breakfast can also help to stabilize blood sugar levels, which can prevent spikes and crashes in energy throughout the day that can lead to fatigue and difficulty concentrating. Consuming healthy fats, such as those found in nuts and avocados, can also help to improve brain function by supporting the production of neurotransmitters and protecting brain cells.

Overall, a nutritious breakfast can provide the brain with the necessary fuel and nutrients to improve focus, attention, and cognitive performance throughout the day.

8. Expressing gratitude as a part of your morning routine can positively impact your mindset and focus. You can accomplish this by either writing down three things you are grateful for in a journal or by sending three text messages to three different people, expressing why they are important to you. This uncomplicated practice can help foster a positive attitude, keep your mind focused on the positives, and improve your emotional and mental well-being throughout the day.

During the Day Routine

1. To optimize your chances of success, it's important to create the ideal environment. Begin by clearing your desk of any unnecessary items and limiting yourself to one open computer program or tab. Play instrumental music or white noise to help sharpen your focus without distracting lyrics. Avoid any music that could divert your attention away from the task at hand.

2. To increase your productivity and concentration, consider dividing your day into time blocks. Designate specific periods for tasks such as checking emails and browsing social media to prevent disruptions. Incorporate the Time Quarter Motion Method, which involves working in 25-minute intervals followed by 5-minute exercise breaks. Utilize this break time to refresh your energy levels and remain focused. Incorporate simple activities like stretching or walking into your breaks for optimal results. See Additional information on the details and benefits of using this method.

3. To become unstoppable, begin with your "why." This entails pinpointing your purpose, passion, and motives for striving towards your objectives. Ask yourself why you're pursuing your goals and what propels you to persevere through challenging times. By gaining a clear comprehension of your "why," you'll possess a potent source of inspiration that can help you remain dedicated and focused on achieving your goals. With a strong enough "why," you can endure any "how."
  Example: "Imagine waking up every morning feeling energized and excited about the day ahead because you know that every action you take is moving you closer to your ultimate purpose. By starting with your 'why,' you'll have a clear and compelling reason to push through any obstacles that come your way."

4. After establishing your "why," the subsequent step is to define particular goals that will enable you to accomplish it. While it's unnecessary to delve into the details of creating SMART goals, as information is widely available, your objectives should be specific, measurable, achievable, and time-bound. Your goals should align with your overall purpose and reflect your desire to achieve them. Example:

Specific: "I want to lose weight."
Measurable: "I want to lose 10 pounds."
Achievable: "I will lose 1-2 pounds per week through a combination of diet and exercise."
Relevant: "Losing weight will improve my overall health and confidence."
Time-bound: "I will reach my goal weight in 10 weeks, by June 1st, 2023."

So, the SMART goal becomes: "I want to lose 10 pounds in 10 weeks, by June 1st, 2023, by losing 1-2 pounds per week through a combination of diet and exercise to improve my overall health and confidence."

5. It's essential to divide significant goals into smaller, achievable steps to monitor your advancement and celebrate successes throughout the process. As my mother always said, "How do you eat an elephant? One bite at a time." Monumental goals can feel intimidating when viewed in their entirety. Therefore, it's critical to break them down into more manageable components and establish actionable steps.

Example: "Set specific goals that are aligned with your purpose. For example, if your purpose is to become a successful entrepreneur, your goals might include launching your first product, generating a certain amount of revenue, or hiring your first employee. By setting specific, measurable goals, you'll be able to track your progress and stay motivated to achieve them."

6. Once you've established smaller, less daunting goals, the next step is to transform them into task lists. The objective is to continue breaking down each goal into specific tasks that can be checked off your list. This approach enables you to visualize each step you're taking and track your progress towards achieving your goals.

7. Once you have created your task list, prioritize your tasks by categorizing them according to their level of importance and urgency, using a system like the Eisenhower Matrix. Evaluate your skills and knowledge to determine which tasks you can handle efficiently and how much time you have available for each task, ensuring you allocate enough time for high-priority tasks. Assign a specific deadline or due date for each task based on its level of importance and urgency and use a calendar or planner to manage your schedule and avoid overcommitting. Identify tasks that can be delegated to others, delegate them to people with the necessary skills and knowledge, and

review the list of tasks to identify any that are unnecessary or can be postponed. Regularly reassess your task list and adjust your priorities as needed to stay focused on the most critical tasks and avoid wasting time on less important ones.

8. To enhance productivity, it's essential to focus on one task at a time. Start by allocating 10-15 minutes to a particular task. Get a piece of paper and create two columns side by side. In one column, list your tasks, and in the other, list the emotions associated with each task. Take a moment to visualize the feeling you'll experience upon achieving each task in the present moment. Imagine it as if you've already completed it and integrated it into your life. Write down these emotions. Every day, add to your feelings list until you've completed the task.

9. I suggest using the Time Quarter Motion Method to tackle your task lists one item at a time. Resist the urge to multitask as it can have a negative impact on your productivity. The human brain is not wired to focus on multiple tasks simultaneously. Attempting to do so divides our attention and forces us to constantly switch between tasks, resulting in a loss of efficiency, increased stress, mental exhaustion, and reduced accuracy. By focusing on one task at a time, you can increase productivity and experience a greater sense of accomplishment. Only move on to the next task once the previous one has been completed.

Evening Routine

1. Take some time to reflect on your day and assess what you have accomplished and what areas require improvement. During this process, consider the following questions:
    a. What aspects of your day worked well?
    b. What didn't go as planned?
    c. What obstacles did you encounter?
    d. What activities or tasks energized you?
    e. What changes should you make to improve your performance?

It's important to regularly review your goals and task list. Merely setting them at the beginning of the year, quarter, or month is insufficient. You should assess them daily and weekly to monitor your progress and determine if adjustments are necessary.

If you notice that you're not making progress towards your goals, take time to analyze why. Perhaps you didn't break your goals down into manageable tasks, or perhaps unforeseeable circumstances have hindered your progress. By reviewing the situation and making adjustments as needed, you can continue to move forward.

2. Prepare for the upcoming day by scheduling your activities and prioritizing tasks according to their significance. Additionally, include any unfinished tasks from the current day's list. It's important to acknowledge that unexpected events can occur, and we may take on more than we can handle. If this happens, ensure that you complete any ongoing tasks before moving on to the next one.

3. Take the time to have dinner with your loved ones, and fully engage in the experience without distractions. This means setting aside all electronic devices, including televisions and smartphones, and focusing solely on the company of those around you.

Sharing meals is an excellent way to connect with others, build relationships, and create lasting memories. Being present during mealtime demonstrates that you value the people in your life and are interested in what they have to say.

Avoiding the temptation to check your phone or browse social media during dinner can enhance your dining experience and promote healthy relationships. Engage in meaningful conversation, listen to what others have to say, and enjoy the nourishing meal before you.

By intentionally setting aside distractions and being present in the moment, you can foster deeper connections with those you care about and create meaningful experiences that will last a lifetime.

4. In order to decompress and promote a restful sleep, consider incorporating physical activity and hydrotherapy into your routine. Going for a walk, soaking in a hot tub, or taking an ice bath can help release tension and relax the body and mind.

Physical activity, such as walking, has been shown to reduce stress levels and improve sleep quality. Similarly, hydrotherapy, which involves immersing the body in water, can help to alleviate muscle soreness, decrease inflammation, and promote relaxation.

Experiment with different techniques to determine what works best for you. You may find that going for a brisk walk in the evening helps to clear your mind and prepare you for a restful night's sleep. Alternatively, soaking in a hot tub or taking a quick dip in an ice bath may help to reduce tension and promote relaxation.

By prioritizing activities that help you decompress and promote restful sleep, you can improve your overall well-being and enjoy greater physical and mental health.

5. In order to promote relaxation and improve the quality of your sleep, it's important to disconnect from technology at least one hour before bedtime. Numerous studies have shown that exposure to electronic devices, such as smartphones, tablets, and laptops, can disrupt sleep patterns and impair cognitive abilities and reaction times.

The average adult requires between 7-9 hours of sleep per night to function optimally. However, the use of technology before bedtime can interfere with the natural sleep cycle, making it more difficult to fall asleep and stay asleep throughout the night.

By disconnecting from technology at least an hour before bedtime, you can promote relaxation and prepare your mind and body for restful sleep. Instead of browsing social media or answering emails, consider engaging in activities that promote relaxation, such as reading a book, practicing meditation, or taking a warm bath.

By prioritizing sleep and establishing healthy sleep habits, you can improve your overall health and well-being, increase productivity, and enhance cognitive function.

6. At the end of each day, take a few minutes to reflect on the positive aspects of your day and write down at least three things you are grateful for. These can be simple things, such as a beautiful sunset, a kind gesture from a friend, or a delicious meal.

By actively focusing on the positive aspects of your life, you can shift your mindset from one of negativity and stress to one of positivity and appreciation. Research has shown that practicing gratitude can lead to a range of benefits, including improved mood, better sleep, increased resilience, and reduced symptoms of depression and anxiety.

Incorporating a gratitude journal into your daily routine is a simple yet powerful way to prioritize positivity and gratitude in your life. By regularly acknowledging the good things in your life, you can cultivate a more positive outlook and improve your overall well-being.

7. Before you go to bed, take a moment to review your task list for the day and reflect on the emotions and feelings associated with each task. Focus on the positive feelings that you desire and let go of any negative emotions or thoughts that may be holding you back. By doing this, you are combining your thoughts, emotions, and desires, and sending clear signals to the universe about your intentions and goals.

Visualize yourself taking action towards achieving your desired outcomes each day, creating a powerful foundation for success. Going to bed with a sense of fulfillment and satisfaction about your goals and desires prompts your subconscious mind to believe in their reality, encouraging you to take action towards achieving them.

Regularly practicing this simple process can help you strengthen your connection to your goals and desires, and develop a greater sense of purpose and direction in your life. By visualizing your desired outcomes and letting go of any negative emotions or thoughts, you can cultivate a more positive and productive mindset, leading to a more fulfilling and meaningful life.

As an example, I personally used this process when I was in the process of purchasing my house. When I made an offer on the house, I took a moment to visualize myself living in the house and stated my intentions for how I wanted to use the space. I pictured myself hosting events that would inspire and motivate people to pursue their dreams and become their best selves.

By focusing on these positive thoughts and feelings, I sent clear signals to the universe about my intentions and goals. Ultimately, this process paid off and I was able to purchase the house. I believe that this was due in part to the power of visualization and positive thinking, as well as the support of whatever higher power or force you believe in.

This experience has shown me the power of using visualization and positive thinking to manifest our desires and achieve our goals. By focusing on what we want and letting go of negative thoughts and emotions, we can align ourselves with the universe and take action towards creating the life we truly desire.

Summary of Daily Routines

Morning Routine Summary

1. Start the day with intention and make your bed.

2. Drink 16 oz of water to hydrate and improve metabolism and digestion.

3. Combine red light therapy, positive motivation, and meditation for 20 minutes to clear your mind and reduce stress.

4. Engage in physical activity to elevate your emotional state and set your mind up for optimal focus.

5. Consider hitting the sauna for 20 minutes after a workout for its various benefits, such as improving blood flow, reducing inflammation, enhancing cardiovascular function, boosting the production of growth hormone, and promoting better mental health.

6. Drink electrolytes after the sauna to restore the balance of essential minerals in the body and prevent dehydration.

7. Eat a nutritional breakfast with complex carbohydrates, protein, and healthy fats to improve focus and concentration throughout the day.

8. Put your phone in airplane mode to limit distractions and cultivate focus and mental clarity.

During The Day Routine Summary

1. Create an ideal work environment

2.Divide your day into time blocks and utilize the Time Quarter Motion Method

3.Start with your "why" and define specific goals

4.Break down significant goals into smaller, achievable steps

5.Transform goals into task lists

6. Prioritize tasks and use a system like the Eisenhower Matrix

7. Focus on one task at a time and avoid multitasking

Evening Routine Summary

1. Reflect on the day and assess accomplishments and areas for improvement.

2. Prepare for the upcoming day by scheduling and prioritizing tasks.

3. Have dinner with loved ones without distractions to connect and build relationships.

4. Incorporate physical activity and hydrotherapy to promote relaxation and restful sleep.

5. Disconnect from technology at least one hour before bedtime to improve sleep quality.

6. Reflect on positive aspects of the day and write down at least three things to be grateful for.

7. Review task list for the day and reflect on positive feelings to set intentions and goals for the future.

Tips

1. Focus on the process, not the outcome. Embrace failure as a learning opportunity.

2. Develop a mindset of abundance and positivity. Practice gratitude daily.

3. Take massive action towards your goals. Focus on progress, not perfection.

4. Embrace the uncomfortable and push yourself beyond your limits.

5. Develop mental toughness and push through pain and discomfort.

6. Practice mindfulness and self-awareness. Focus on living in the present moment.

7. Practice meditation and self-reflection to cultivate inner peace and balance.

8. Embrace discipline and accountability. Hold yourself to high standards.

9. Focus on continuous learning and self-improvement. Prioritize long-term goals over short-term gains.

Remember, achieving a focused outcome requires consistent effort and dedication. By incorporating these practices into your daily routine, you can improve your focus and achieve your goals.

What Happens When You Don't Have Focus in Your Life

Focus is one of the most powerful tools in your arsenal for achieving success and living a fulfilled life. When you are focused, you have a clear path forward. You recognize the direction you're heading and how you plan to get there.

But what happens when you don't have a focus in your life? Believe me; it can be quite a challenge. Without a clear focus, you're like a ship without a rudder. You're aimlessly drifting through life, wondering where you're headed or how you will get there.

It isn't easy to stay on task when your focus is lacking. You go from one thing to the next, never sticking to it or completing your plans. You might have a lot of great ideas, but with focus, you'll be able to turn those ideas into reality.

An inability to focus can also lead to feeling overwhelmed and stressed. You might have so many things on your plate that you need help figuring out where to start or what to prioritize. This can leave you feeling frustrated and anxious, and it isn't easy to make any actual progress toward your goals.

How can you regain your focus when it's slipping away? Identifying what's causing the lack of focus is the opening step. For example, do you feel you have too many tasks to manage? Is it a challenge for you to say no to disruptions? Do you need a sense of direction or purpose in your life?

You can make changes when you know what is causing your lack of focus. This may include setting specific targets and objectives, forming a timetable or routine to help you stay on course, or practicing mindfulness and meditation to assist you in remaining focused and present.

Keep in mind that focus is a critical part of success and satisfaction. Don't let a lack of focus hold you back from achieving your dreams and living your desired life. By doing the work and having the right mindset, you can create the focus to bring your goals to life.

When your attention is focused, it can become easier to make progress in your plans and find fulfillment in your everyday life. However, if you need a clear idea of which way to go, you may feel stuck or not knowing which steps to take next, causing a feeling of apathy or losing interest.

Self-Assessment Focus Trait Questions

• How often do you find yourself easily distracted by external factors, such as noise or interruptions?

• When working on a task, how often do you lose track of time or get completely absorbed in what you are doing?

• How well do you manage your time and prioritize your daily tasks? Do you clearly understand what needs to be done and when, or do you tend to procrastinate or become overwhelmed by your workload?

• How often do you multitask or try to work on several tasks simultaneously? Do you find that this approach helps or hinders your ability to focus?

• How do you handle distractions or interruptions when they do arise? Can you quickly refocus on the task at hand, or do these factors completely derail your progress?

• How do you stay motivated and engaged when working on tasks that may be less interesting or challenging? Do you find ways to stay focused and energized or become bored and disengaged?

• How do you approach technology and other digital devices in your work and personal life? Do you find that these tools help or hinder your ability to focus?

• How do you manage your physical environment to support your ability to focus? Do certain settings or conditions help you stay focused and productive?

• How do you handle stress and pressure when working on tasks requiring high focus and attention? Do you find that these factors help or hinder your ability to concentrate?

• How would you rate your overall ability to focus on tasks and stay productive throughout the day? Can you consistently achieve your goals and meet your deadlines, or do you struggle to stay on track?

Your Focus Action Steps

1. Set clear goals. Define your goals and make them specific, measurable, achievable, relevant, and time-bound. Write them down to keep yourself accountable.

2. Prioritize tasks. Make a list of all the tasks you need to complete and prioritize them based on their urgency and importance.

3. Break tasks into smaller steps. Break down your tasks into smaller, manageable steps to make them less overwhelming and easier to accomplish.

4. Create a schedule. Plan your day or week in advance, and block off time for specific tasks. This will help you stay on track and avoid distractions.

5. Eliminate distractions. Remove any distractions that may hinder your focus, such as turning off your phone or closing unnecessary tabs on your computer.

6. Take breaks. Give yourself time to rest and recharge. Take short breaks after completing a task or set a timer for a 5–10-minute break every hour.

7. Practice mindfulness. Practice being present in the moment and focus on the task at hand. This can help reduce stress and increase productivity.

8. Get organized. Keep your workspace clean and organized, and make sure you have all the necessary tools and resources within reach.

9. Stay motivated. Stay motivated by reminding yourself of your goals and celebrating small successes along the way.

10. Evaluate your progress. Regularly evaluate your progress and adjust your approach as needed to improve your focus and achieve your goals.

TRAIT #2: R = RESILIENCE

"Be like water making its way through cracks. Do not be assertive, but adjust to the object, and you shall find a way around or through it. If nothing within you stays rigid, outward things will disclose themselves. Empty your mind, be formless. Shapeless, like water. If you put water into a cup, it becomes the cup. You put water into a bottle and it becomes the bottle. You put it in a teapot, it becomes the teapot. Now, water can flow or it can crash. Be water, my friend." - Bruce Lee

What is it to be Resilient?

To be resilient means to can recover quickly from challenging situations, adapt to change, and bounce back from adversity or setbacks. Resilience is the capacity to face and overcome obstacles, persevere in the face of difficulty, and maintain a positive outlook and a sense of purpose even when faced with significant stress or adversity.

What is Resilience?

Resilience is the ability to keep going despite adversity, despite all odds and obstacles. It is a quality that allows us to overcome our circumstances and achieve our goals regardless of what life throws. Being resilient means picking yourself up after falling hard and never giving up on your dreams, even when everything around you tells you it's impossible. We can develop resilience through practice, determination, and self-awareness; by developing these qualities, we can learn how to stay motivated during difficult times and become stronger than ever. We must take charge of our lives and learn how to adapt during challenging times to remain focused on our overall objectives.

Hard work and dedication forge resilience. It starts with developing a strong self-awareness and understanding that we are in control of our lives, regardless of our circumstances. Next, we must learn to identify and recognize when we feel overwhelmed or frustrated to take the necessary steps to move forward. Resilience also requires developing healthy coping mechanisms, such as engaging in positive activities, resting properly, and taking breaks when needed. Finally, resilience means having an optimistic outlook on life even during tough times, believing that you will get through this challenging period, and finding ways to stay motivated even when things seem impossible.

Resilience is not just about surviving but thriving despite difficulty. It is about pushing past the adverse circumstances of life and emerging as a better, more empowered person. Resilience gives us the courage to never give up and keep going, no matter what. We can make our lives whatever we want them to be with resilience! So don't let anyone or anything stop you from living your best life; develop your resilience and show you have the strength to overcome any obstacle!

By developing resilience, you are taking ownership of yourself and your future. You are committing yourself that nothing will stand in your way–not even your pain and suffering. Know that you have the capability and power within you to become stronger, more intelligent, more successful, and happier than ever before. You can make your dreams a reality; no one can take that away from you. So, take charge of your life, develop resilience, and show you are the ultimate underdog!

Having resilience is the key to continuing, no matter what obstacle you face. Practice and stay determined, but if you put in enough effort and understanding, you can figure out how to handle hard times without letting go. We must keep our eyes on the prize no matter what comes our way, be aware of when we need help, and stay motivated even during difficult times. If we remain committed, we can shape our lives into whatever we wish them to be;

It won't be a piece of cake, but with enough dedication, knowledge of yourself, and perseverance, you can learn to be more resilient. Have faith in yourself, don't give up, and eventually, you'll get to show everyone that no matter how many times life knocks you down, you'll still get up and keep on going. Don't shy away from any challenge - face it head-on, and you will succeed! Everything you need to make your dreams a reality is already inside you. Demonstrate how resilient you are by standing up for what you believe is right.

Being resilient doesn't mean you don't feel stress or struggle with difficult emotions, but you can learn to control those emotions and stay hopeful, no matter what comes your way.

My Personal Story About Being Resilient

Let's talk about resiliency. Now, I know what you're thinking, "Oh great, another boring talk about bouncing back from failure." But wait, let me tell you a brief tale of a small-legged, energetic college track athlete. I wasn't the quickest person on the track. But I had a secret weapon. No, it's not a fancy pair of shoes or a high-tech training program. It's my lower center of gravity and my ability to laugh in the face of adversity. With my short legs, I was lower to the ground like a sports car, which made me perfect for running the curve in the 200 meters. I was determined to make an impression in my first college track meet.

I was crushing it, coming out of the curve, leaving all the tall people in the dust, and feeling like a champion. Then, as I got the straightaway, I felt a sharp pain in my hamstring without any warning; I pulled my hamstring. While lying there, I saw my dad sprinting towards me faster than someone who's really hungry at an all-you-can-eat restaurant. He helped me make it to the finish line, teaching me a valuable lesson: finish what you start. Even though I didn't win, I realized that genuine success isn't about the destination; it's about the experience and the people who help us along the way.

Over the next four years, I faced many challenges and obstacles. But I never let that stop me from pushing forward. I may not have had the most successful career on the track, but I never gave up. I finally participated in the conference championships during my senior year, and it was one of the most rewarding experiences of my life. I didn't have a successful showing in the 100 meters, 200 meters, 400 meters, and the 4x100 meter relay team.

One of my teammates I trained with was running the 400-meter hurdles, and I was the secret weapon he relied on. I was the secret weapon that pushed him to greatness. What I mean by a rabbit is, have you ever seen a dog chase after a rabbit? The dog is relentless and won't give up until it catches it. He would run the hurdles, and I was the rabbit he chased after. He was victorious in the 400-meter hurdles at the conference championships. It's essential to keep in mind that even if you doubt the impact you are having, you are still making one. Your dedication and effort can assist others in accomplishing their aspirations and unlocking their fullest potential.

Before I could compete as a college athlete, I needed to pass the

NCAA Prop 48 rule, which made me initially ineligible. As a freshman athlete, I didn't meet the necessary ACT and SAT standards. I needed a 2.3 GPA and pass 24 credit hours to practice with the team. As I worked to achieve this objective, I discovered I had specific learning impairments, particularly numbers dyscalculia, which caused me to transpose digits when under pressure; processing speed dysgraphia, where I could not keep up with the pace of my thought processes, and expressive language disorder, which made it difficult for me to articulate my ideas.

Battling my learning disabilities was challenging, but it helped me better understand resilience and determination. I had to study and take tests fitting my particular learning style to succeed. I acquired cliff notes for each course to grasp the essentials and screen out any unneeded information. When I had to read something, I jotted it down and asked myself what the passage was trying to show me. To get past my struggles with math, I took my time and checked and rechecked my work, as I had a habit of switching numbers when I was feeling overwhelmed. I conversed with my professors and defended my right to partial credit when I knew I had merited it. I employed a tutor to teach me improved study habits and comprehend the subjects quicker, and I asked my classmates for their outlook on how they reached their answers. It was a challenge to cultivate the state of mind to adjust and persist, but I realized that real fortitude is not about never falling but about getting back up and going ahead. Whatever roadblocks come in your path. Keeping a positive outlook and working diligently can help us overcome barriers and reach our ambitions.

True resilience doesn't just mean enduring hard times and sadness; it also means finding joy even in challenging situations. No matter what has happened—whether it's a job loss, the death of a loved one, a failed competition, or an injury—how you handle it will make you wiser and stronger. For example, it devastated me when I got laid off from my first job. But then, I changed my mindset and realized it was just business.

My friends, don't let anyone or anything keep you from reaching your highest potential. Embrace your strengths and make them work for you. Learn to find humor in difficult situations and look for growth opportunities in your challenges. When you meet a setback, get back up and keep pushing forward with determination and perseverance. Remember that the real victory is not in reaching a destination; it is in the journey and the help of those who help us achieve it. Giving moral support to others as they embark on their journey.

Remember to value the potential of your ambition and desire to succeed. You have the power to do extraordinary things, and you can triumph over any hurdle that appears in your path. Believe in yourself and your talents, and never abandon your ambitions. Find individuals who will support your dreams and success, as well as seek to help others reach their goals. As a team, anything we set out to do is within our reach. So let's take a step forward with courage and create the life we've always envisioned.

Now that I've shared my resiliency experience, let's dig deeper into the different methods that use it as a superpower.

Tap Into Your Resilience
For Positive Transformation

There are lots of options for increasing your resilience. One way is to identify your strengths and weaknesses. This can help you determine which aspects of your life need improvement to build resilience. Please ensure the goals you set for yourself are achievable, and be prepared to try to reach them. During difficult times, having a support system of family and friends who can provide encouragement and assistance is beneficial. Here are some easy methods to get back on track after any setbacks.

Focus on What You Can Control

Listen up, folks. It's time to get real. Some things in life are simply out of our control, and we need to keep a clear perspective on this fact. But here's the thing - that doesn't mean we should throw in the towel and give up. No way.

Instead, it's time to focus on what we can control and take responsibility for. Take a good, hard look at your situation and determine what you can do to make a difference. Save time and energy on things beyond your power - that's a recipe for feeling overwhelmed and burnt out.

The key here is accountability. Own up to what you can change, and make a plan of action to tackle it head-on. This will help you to prioritize, and to use your energy on what matters. In addition, by focusing on what you can control, you can take practical steps towards making progress and achieving your goals. That's what it's all about, baby!

And here's another thing - focusing on what you can control doesn't just help you progress. It also helps you to maintain a positive attitude and stay motivated in the face of challenges. Constantly trying to control things that are out of your control can lead to frustration, stress, and negative emotions. But when you focus on what you can control, you feel more in charge of your life, which can be a powerful motivator.

So, let's get real and take ownership of our lives. Don't let the things you can't control bring you down. Instead, focus on what you can do, plan, and take action. Keep your eyes on the prize, and you'll be amazed at what you can achieve.

Control Your Reaction

Let's take a moment to reflect on how we respond to setbacks. Do we let them defeat us, or do we become even more determined to achieve success? Do we take ownership of the setback or blame others for our misfortune?

It's important to be honest with ourselves and look at our response. Are we dedicated to overcoming obstacles and finding solutions, or are we ready to throw in the towel at the first sign of difficulty? Do we let anger and frustration consume us or maintain a calm and peaceful mindset?

Remember, blaming others or getting angry will not solve the problem. But, taking ownership of the situation and focusing on finding a solution will. So, let's strive to stay calm and centered in the face of setbacks. Let's focus on what we can control and take proactive steps towards achieving our goals. With determination and a peaceful mindset, we can overcome any obstacle and achieve our desired success.

Examine the Situation and Use It as a Learning Opportunity

Alright, it's time to get analytical! When facing a setback, it's important to take a step back and analyze what went wrong. This will help us identify what we can do differently to increase our chances of success. So, let's ask ourselves the following questions:

Firstly, did we have the wrong approach? If so, what approach should we have taken instead? Secondly, did we need to gain the necessary skills or knowledge to succeed? What steps can we take to acquire the required skills and expertise if that is the case?

Lastly, let's ask ourselves what happened and how we can be better prepared for similar situations. By examining the setback and finding ways to improve, we'll be better equipped to handle similar situations.

Remember, setbacks are not failures. They're opportunities for growth and improvement. By reflecting on what went wrong and how we can do better in the future, we'll increase our chances of success and become more resilient in the face of challenges. So, let's embrace setbacks as opportunities for growth and use them to become better, stronger, and more successful.

Take a Breath

Alright, let's take a moment to catch our breath and regroup. It's important to remember that it's better to take a brief pause before tackling any challenge. Taking a moment to recenter and refocus can help us approach the situation with a clear and calm mindset.

Remember, the problem you're facing will still be there tomorrow. You have 24 hours to process your defeat, learn from it, and allow yourself to feel disappointed. But after that, it's time to get back to work and not dwell on the setback any longer.

Don't let setbacks define you or hold you back from achieving your goals. Instead, use them as motivation to learn, grow, and become even stronger. So, take a deep breath, reset your mindset, and get back to work. The road to success may have obstacles, but with determination and a positive attitude, you can overcome them and achieve greatness.

Make a New Plan

Great job! You gave it your best shot and encountered a setback but didn't give up. You took the time to recover and learn from your mistakes; now it's time to try again.

Remember, repeating this process is vital to achieving success. It's essential to take a step back, analyze what went wrong, and then develop a new and improved plan to move forward. Ask yourself the following questions:

- *What is your new and improved plan?*
- *Why do you believe this plan will work better than the last time?*
- *What actions can you take today to start implementing your plan?*

Ensure your plan is realistic and something you can commit to for the long haul. Avoid making plans requiring weeks or months of preparation before starting. Instead, focus on taking action today and making progress toward your goal.

Remember, setbacks are a natural part of the process. It's how you respond to them that determines your ultimate success. By learning from your mistakes and staying committed to your goal, you can achieve anything you set your mind to. So, let's get back to work and make it happen!

Manage Your Mindset

How's your mental state right now? Are you feeling desperate or determined? Are you confident in your abilities, or are you feeling hopeless?

It's important to check in with yourself and assess your mindset. A negative mindset can suggest that you don't fully trust your plan. To combat this, ensure you have a plan that makes you feel confident.

Your plan should be realistic, achievable, and challenging enough to push you outside your comfort zone. Ensure you have specific, measurable goals aligned with your overall vision. Finally, and most importantly, make sure you believe in yourself and your ability to achieve your goals.

Remember, your mindset plays a crucial role in your success. You can overcome obstacles and achieve your wildest dreams by staying positive, focused, and determined. So, let's develop a mindset of unwavering confidence and start progressing towards your goals!

Realize How Strong You Are

In your DNA is the resilience and strength of your ancestors who faced and conquered unimaginable challenges. Remember that you are not just an ordinary person, but the product of a lineage of survivors. Today's difficulties are insignificant compared to what your forefathers had to endure. You have the power within you to overcome any obstacle or adversity. Embrace the strength and resilience in your genes and use it to push through any hardship. With every challenge, you are tapping into the same force that runs in your blood. Believe in yourself and your ability to conquer anything life throws your way.

Embrace Positivity and Success

Be optimistic and strive for success. Believe in yourself and your ability to overcome any obstacle or setback. Remember, setbacks are just opportunities to become more focused and determined. Create a plan and commit to it, reminding yourself that you will not give up until you have achieved the life you desire. Give yourself permission to be powerful and take control of your life. Believe that you can do it, and take the necessary actions to make it happen. Don't let setbacks hold you back; instead, use them as a stepping stone toward your ultimate goal. It's important to remember that setbacks are a normal part of the journey, so don't beat yourself up if it happens. Learn from it and move forward with even greater determination.

Persevere

No matter how many times you fail, don't ever give up! With grit, determination, and a positive attitude, you can overcome any setback that comes your way. Remember, quitting is never an option to achieve your goals. Instead, keep pushing through the tough times, and don't lose sight of your dreams. Failure is not the opposite of success; it's part of the journey. Use every setback as an opportunity to learn, grow, and come back stronger.

Some people might be naturally more resilient than others, but you can still work on building your resilience. By putting in some effort and self-management, you can become a more resilient version of yourself. And let me tell you, the more resilient you are, the more successful you'll be! There are many ways to enhance your personal growth, but building your resilience is definitely one avenue worth considering. So, keep your head up, stay determined, and watch your success grow!

Ways To Increase Resilience Summary

1. Identify personal strengths and weaknesses

2. Set achievable goals and be prepared to put in the effort to reach them

3. Build a support system of family and friends

4. Focus on what you can control

5. Control your reaction by taking ownership of the situation and focusing on finding a solution

6. Examine the situation and use it as a learning opportunity

7. Take a breath to recenter and refocus

8. Make a new plan to move forward and try again.

What Happens When You Don't
Have Resiliency in Your Life

Let's face it; life can be challenging. We all experience losses, setbacks, and adversity. But here's the thing, you need more resilience to bounce back. You may find yourself overwhelmed by stress, anxiety, and negative emotions. And let's be honest, who wants that?

Not having resilience means you struggle to adjust to changes and unpredictable situations. That job loss, relationship challenges, or health problems? Yeah, it's going to strike you. But it doesn't have to be that way.

When you lack resilience, achieving your goals and pursuing your passions becomes monumental. As a result, you feel discouraged, and giving up feels like the only option when faced with obstacles or setbacks. But trust me; it doesn't have to be that way.

The bottom line is not having resilience in your life can have a massive impact on your mental health, relationships, and overall quality of life. But don't despair! Resilience is a skill that you can develop and master over time.

By cultivating a strong support system, taking care of yourself, reframing negative thoughts, and developing a growth mindset, you can become more resilient and better equipped to cope with life's challenges. Resilience is the key to navigating life's ups and downs with grace and strength.

So, don't let a lack of resilience hold you back. Instead, it's time to build a foundation for success and fulfillment. With a positive attitude, a commitment to self-improvement, and a willingness to push through discomfort, you can become a master of resilience.

Self-Assessment Resilient Trait Questions

• How do you typically respond to setbacks or obstacles in your life? Do you tend to give up easily, or do you find ways to bounce back and persevere?

• How do you manage stress and adversity in your daily life? Do you have strategies for coping with difficult situations and emotions?

• How well do you adapt to change and uncertainty? Can you adjust your plans and expectations when circumstances change, or are you overwhelmed and stuck in your ways?

• How do you view failure and mistakes? Do you see them as opportunities for growth and learning, or do you become discouraged and defeated when things don't go as planned?

• How do you maintain a positive outlook and hope, even when facing difficult circumstances? Do you find ways to stay optimistic or become overwhelmed by negative thoughts and emotions?

• How do you draw on your past experiences and strengths to help you navigate challenges in the present? Do you have a sense of resilience from past successes and achievements?

• How do you nurture your physical, emotional, and spiritual well-being to help you stay resilient? Do you prioritize self-care and relaxation, even during stress and adversity?

• How do you seek out support and guidance when facing difficult situations? Do you have a network of people who can offer encouragement and advice?

• How do you stay motivated and focused on your goals, even when facing obstacles and setbacks? Do you have a clear sense of purpose and direction that helps you stay committed and driven?

• How would you rate your resilience and ability to bounce back from challenges and setbacks? Do you feel you can handle adversity with strength and grace, or do you struggle to stay resilient in the face of difficulty?

Your Resilient Action Steps

1. Accept change: Recognize that change is a natural part of life and that it is okay to feel uncomfortable or uncertain about it.

2. Practice positive self-talk: Encourage yourself with positive self-talk to build resilience and maintain a positive attitude even in difficult situations.

3. Cultivate a support network: Surround yourself with supportive people who can provide encouragement and help you navigate challenging situations.

4. Focus on your strengths: Identify your strengths and use them to your advantage. This can help you build confidence and resilience.

5. Set realistic goals: Set achievable goals that align with your values and priorities. This can help you stay focused and motivated, even in difficult times.

6. Stay flexible: Be willing to adjust your plans as needed to adapt to changing circumstances. This can help you stay resilient and avoid feeling stuck.

7. Practice self-care: Take care of yourself physically, mentally, and emotionally. Get enough sleep, eat healthily, exercise regularly, and take breaks when you need them.

8. Learn from failures: Instead of viewing failure as a negative, use it as an opportunity to learn and grow. This can help you build resilience and become more resilient.

9. Stay optimistic: Maintain a positive outlook and focus on the good things in your life, even when things are tough. This can help you stay resilient and overcome challenges.

10. Practice gratitude: Express gratitude for the people, experiences, and things in your life. This can help you maintain a positive perspective and build resilience.

TRAIT #3: E = ENERGETIC

The energy of the mind is the essence of life. -Aristotle

What is it to be Energetic?

To be energetic means to have a high level of physical or mental activity and vitality. It is feeling lively, active, and enthusiastic, with a strong desire to take on and accomplish tasks or activities.

Physical energy can be seen through speed and intensity, feeling alert and awake, and strong endurance. Mental energy, on the other hand, can be seen through traits such as quick thinking, intense focus, and a positive attitude toward new challenges.

Being energetic can also be characterized by enthusiasm and passion, particularly for things one enjoys or is passionate about. This helps sustain and increase energy levels over time, even during tasks or activities that might be physically or mentally challenging.

Overall, being energetic is a state of high activity, enthusiasm, and vitality that can help to increase productivity, motivation, and overall well-being.

What is Energy?

We often think of energy in terms of physical activity or enthusiasm, but the concept of energy goes much deeper. We are energetic human beings, vibrating with energy, and everything around us is made up of energy. We cannot create nor destroy this energy – it transforms from one form to another. However, we can tap into this energy and use it for our benefit. We all have access to the unlimited potential that comes from the energetic force of the universe.

We can use this energy to create anything we set our minds to, from material possessions to emotional and spiritual well-being. We can access this energy simply by connecting to it through meditation, visualization, and other practices. This energy is the foundation of our entire universe, and by understanding its potential, we can tap into its power and use it to our advantage. We can manifest abundance in all areas of our lives and make the most out of this incredible force that surrounds and sustains us. We are energetic human beings, and we have the potential to create anything with the power of energy.

It is important to become aware of our energy and the power that lies within it. We all have access to the same energy source, so why not use it to our benefit? We can tap into this energy to manifest abundance and create our desired life. We all have the power to make the most out of this incredible force, and by understanding it, we can make the most out of our lives. We are energetic human beings, capable of creating anything with the power of energy. We need to tap into it and use it wisely.

As we strive for an unstoppable mindset, we must recognize the energy we possess and learn how to harness it to manifest abundance and create the life we desire. My journey with energy has taught me the power of tapping into this source, and I'd like to share it with you now.

My Personal Story About Being Energetic

The first time I truly understood the power of energy was when my mother was on her deathbed. I was sitting by her side, holding her hand and whispering words of comfort, creating a safe and peaceful space for her to transition. I realized then that death is not the end but a new beginning for those who believe.

As I sat there, I remembered a technique I had learned from a past partner, a form of energy healing called Reiki. I gently placed my hands over my mother's body, channeling healing energy to her. To my surprise, as I touched her hand, I felt a surge of energy travel through my body, from my fingertips to my arm, and finally, a powerful shock near my heart. It was as if my mother was giving me one last gift, the gift of her energy.

Since that day, I have been on a spiritual journey to learn everything I can about energy. I have come to understand that energy is everything. The life force flows through all of us and the universe. When we die, our energy does not die with us, it returns to the universe. We are all connected by this energy, which constantly flows and exchanges between us.

I have also learned that two types of energies exist within us, masculine and feminine, similar to the concept of yin and yang in Chinese philosophy. Masculine energy is logical, direct, and conquering, whereas feminine energy is creative, nurturing, and refined. Both energies are present within us and finding balance between them is essential. We need to draw on both types of energy to be balanced.

We need the masculine energy to help us make logical decisions, take action and achieve our goals. But, at the same time, we also need the feminine energy to help us connect with our emotions, nurture our relationships and be creative.

When out of balance, we may experience negative emotions and struggle to achieve our goals. For example, if we have too much masculine energy, we may become rigid, controlling and struggle to connect with our emotions. On the other hand, if we have more feminine energy, we may become more active, more confident and able to take action.

To find balance, it's essential to become aware of which energy we are currently drawing on and consciously incorporate the other energy. This can be done through practices like meditation, journaling, and self-reflection.

By understanding and harnessing the power of both masculine and feminine energy within us, we can achieve balance and live a fulfilling life. Ultimately, it's all about finding the right balance between these energies, similar to yin and yang, where the balance between the two creates harmony.

However, as we age, we often lose sight of this truth of the energies, similar to the concept of yin and yang in Chinese philosophy. Society and our life conditioning can cause us to become disconnected from our true essence. Children, for example, have an innate sense of truth because they are naturally connected to their energy and can sense the vibrations of those around them. They are open, loving, and have a limitless sense of possibilities. They have not yet been programmed with limited beliefs as well they are not hiding behind masks putting up fake images of themselves wanting to be liked, loved and validated.

To find balance, it is important to become aware of which energy we are currently drawing on and make a conscious effort to incorporate the other energy. This can be done through practices like meditation, journaling, and self-reflection. By understanding and harnessing the power of both masculine and feminine energy within us, similar to the concept of yin and yang, where the balance between the two creates harmony, we can achieve balance and live a fulfilling life. It's important to find balance between these energies, rather than trying to fit into societal expectations of masculinity or femininity.

To have positive energy is to allow it to flow without resistance. Unfortunately, this energy resistance comes in many forms: limited beliefs, ego, control, attachments, expectations, debt, stress, past traumas, mental disorders, doubt, uncertainty and addictions. These things can prevent us from shining our true light and living abundantly.

As I reflect on my mother and the powerful gift of energy she gave me, I am reminded of the profound realization that energy is not just something that can be harnessed for healing purposes. Still, it is also a fundamental aspect of our existence. It connects us all and is the force that flows through us, the universe, and everything in between. Our responsibility is to use it wisely and strive for balance in our lives and interactions with others. By understanding and harnessing the power of energy, we can overcome energy resistance and live a life filled with love, peace, and abundance. Let us strive to be like children, open and connected to the energy surrounding us, and allow it to flow freely without resistance. I am grateful for the lessons I have learned and the understanding I have gained about the importance of energy in our lives and hope to inspire others to explore the power of energy and strive for balance in their lives.

Having heard my personal story about energy, let's focus on the practical steps to access and harness your energy to reach your goals and manifest abundance.

It's important to recognize that emotions are a means of communication from your subconscious, not necessarily objective truth. While it's valid to feel emotions in response to different situations, it's crucial to not always act on them, especially when they don't serve you. Developing the skill of overriding emotions can be essential in navigating life.

While emotions can be powerful, it's important to recognize that they may not always reflect reality. Instead of being governed by emotions, it's important to master and manage them. Mindfulness of thoughts is crucial in manifesting what you desire, as negative thoughts can lead to negative emotions and outcomes. It's essential to choose positive thoughts to manifest positive emotions and experiences intentionally. It's important to retrain the ego to hold onto positives and release negatives to avoid holding onto trauma.

Energy is the Essence to Your Life

As an energetic being living a human experience, a person's mindset and mental resistance can significantly impact how they see, live, and experience the world around them. In addition, our mindset and mental resistance can shape our beliefs, attitudes, and perceptions, ultimately affecting our behavior and actions.

For instance, a person with a growth mindset may view challenges and setbacks as opportunities for growth and learning, leading them to approach life with greater resilience, optimism, and a sense of possibility. On the other hand, a person with a fixed mindset may feel defeated by challenges and setbacks, leading them to adopt a more negative attitude and view the world as more rigid and limiting.

Mind resistance can profoundly impact an individual's capacity to engage fully with others and experience the world around them, ultimately hindering the soul from radiating its brilliance.

When we resist or push against our thoughts, emotions, and experiences, we can create unnecessary tension and stress, making it more difficult to present and engage in the present moment fully. By cultivating mindfulness and acceptance, we can reduce mind resistance and create a more peaceful and fulfilling way of experiencing life.

A person's mindset and mind resistance can greatly impact their operating system and worldview. Individuals who develop a growth mindset and decrease their mental resistance can lead more gratifying and purposeful lives. An individual's operating system comprises various components, such as their beliefs, values, thoughts, emotions, and physical state. These components shape how a person perceives and interacts with the world around them, influencing their behavior, decisions, and overall well-being.

The mind can create resistance that can inhibit our ability to live a fulfilling life. Many factors, such as not knowing our value, low standards, not being mindful, and negative thoughts, can contribute to mental resistance and prevent us from fully experiencing the present moment.

External factors such as stress, negative people, and limited beliefs can also contribute to mental resistance and hinder our ability to live fulfilling lives.

On the other hand, practicing gratitude, taking care of our physical body, seeking support when needed, being open to change, and letting go of expectations can all help reduce mental resistance and promote a more fulfilling way of life.

It is important to note that while these practices can be helpful, each individual's journey to reducing mental resistance and finding fulfillment is unique and may require different approaches. Therefore, it is essential to listen to our inner guidance and seek out support to help us along the way.

The mind resistance combines several factors, including limiting beliefs, negative thoughts, stress, lack of mindfulness, and self-care. Reducing mind resistance is crucial to increasing energy levels, motivation, focus, and engagement. The relationship between mind resistance and energy is significant, as lowering mind resistance can increase personal energy levels.

This chapter will discuss various methods to decrease mind resistance and increase personal energy levels. By implementing these practices, we can reduce limiting beliefs, eliminate negative thoughts, manage stress, and improve mindfulness and self-care. The ultimate goal is to increase our energy levels and feel more alive and engaged daily.

Therefore, by exploring different ways to limit mind resistance, we can increase our energy levels and improve our overall quality of life. This chapter will provide practical tips and strategies to incorporate into our daily routines to overcome mind resistance and unleash the power of energy in our lives.

1. Know your value. Your values can have a significant impact on your energy in your life. When your values are aligned with your actions and decisions, it provides a sense of purpose and meaning that energizes and motivates you.

2. Raising your standards can positively affect a person's personal energy by providing motivation, focus, and a sense of accomplishment and helping to build resilience.

3. Practice mindfulness and being present in the moment. This can help you let go of resistance and attachments and allow energy to flow more freely.

4. Take care of your physical body. Exercise, eat healthy, and get enough sleep to help your body and mind function at their best.

5. Power of Positive Thinking. This can help you let go of negative beliefs and patterns that block energy flow.

6. Let go of the need to control things outside of your control. This can help you reduce resistance and stress.

7. Practice gratitude and focus on the positive aspects of your life. This can help you shift your perspective and allow more positive energy to flow.

8. Seek support and help when needed. If you are struggling with traumas, mental disorders, or addictions, it can be helpful to seek professional help to address these issues and allow energy to flow more freely.

9. Surround yourself with positive, supportive people. Being around positive energy can help you cultivate more positive energy in your own life.

10. Eliminate limited beliefs; these negative thoughts and ideas are holding back your true potential and ability to achieve your goals.

11. Reduce stress; stress can be a major source of resistance in your life. Finding ways to manage and reduce stress, such as through techniques, exercise, or talking to a trusted friend or therapist, can help you let go of the resistance and allow more positive energy to flow.

12. Be open to change; reduce your attachment to a specific outcome and be more adaptable to new situations. Attachment to an outcome can affect a person's energy in several ways. If you are very attached to a particular outcome, you may feel a lot of pressure to achieve it, which can be stressful and draining. This stress can deplete your energy levels and make it more challenging to focus on other tasks. On the other hand, if you can let go of your attachment to a specific outcome and focus on the process instead, you may feel less stressed and more energized. It's essential to find a balance between having goals and being attached to the outcome and learning to be flexible and adaptable to maintain a healthy energy level.

13. Quieting your ego, so you can hear your truth of inner wisdom. Your ego can have a significant effect on your personal energy. The ego is part of the self that is concerned with one's own interests and views, and it can influence how a person thinks, feels, and behaves.

14. Let go of expectations. Expectations can have a significant effect on a person's energy levels. For example, we may feel motivated and energized with high expectations of ourselves or others. On the other hand, if we have

low expectations, we may feel demotivated and less energetic. Additionally, unrealistic expectations may make us feel overwhelmed and stressed, which can drain our energy. Therefore, it's important to set realistic expectations for ourselves and others to maintain a healthy energy level.

Remember that it takes time and effort to apply energy to your life, but with practice and patience, you can make positive changes that can lead to a more energetic, fulfilling life and it starts with knowing your value.

The Secret to Knowing Your Value

In today's society, there is a pervasive belief that a person's value is linked to financial success, status, and material possessions. This notion is reinforced by various forms of media, including social media, TV shows, movies, and advertisements. As a result, wealthy and accomplished individuals are often glorified as being content and fulfilled. Yet, at the same time, those with fewer resources or lower status are depicted as less valuable or less happy.

Individuals can internalize these cultural messages and contribute to feelings of inadequacy or low self-worth if they don't measure up to these cultural expectations. However, it's important to recognize that cultural messages and cultural expectations, as well as financial success, status and possessions do not determine a person's true worth and value as a human being. A person's inherent value is not determined by external factors or cultural perceptions, but rather by the person.

One way to determine a person's value is through personal beliefs, morals, ethics, and integrity, as these elements reflect their character and principles. But this is just one perspective, and value is a subjective measure that may differ for different people.

Personal beliefs, morals, ethics, and integrity are essential aspects that reflect a person's character and principles. These values shape an individual's decision-making process, relationships, and world perception. As a result, those around them often view someone who embodies these values as trustworthy, reliable, and respectable.

However, determining a person's value is subjective and can differ depending on the individual and the context. For example, one person may value financial success and material possessions, while another may prioritize personal growth and self-fulfillment. In addition, some may value family and relationships over professional success, while others may prioritize their career over personal relationships.

Moreover, a person's value may evolve as they grow and learn from their experiences. As individuals encounter new situations and challenges, their beliefs, morals, and ethics may be tested, and they may need to re-evaluate their values and principles.

Ultimately, determining a person's value is a complex matter that cannot be reduced to external factors such as financial success or social status. While personal beliefs, morals, ethics, and integrity provide some insight into an individual's character and principles, it is important to recognize that value is subjective and can vary depending on the individual and their context.

With that in mind, let me provide an example strategy for identifying your values.

First, you must determine your values to live a fulfilling life. Your values are the foundation upon which you build your life. Your values are the guiding principles that dictate your behavior, decisions, and ultimately, your destiny. So, it's crucial to take the time to reflect and identify what truly matters to you.

To start, think about your experiences. Your experiences shape your values. Think about the moments when you felt most fulfilled, happy, and satisfied. What values were important to you in those moments? This will give you a good starting point to identify your core values.

Next, consider your beliefs. Beliefs are the hidden forces that shape our lives. What do you believe in, and why? What are your guiding principles? This will help you understand the values most important to you.

It's also essential to reflect on your priorities. You have to prioritize to make progress. What are the most important aspects of your life? How do you allocate your time and energy towards them? Life is a battle between your priorities and your distractions. Use the Life Energy Wheel to assess the balance in your life. If the wheel appears imbalanced, you must prioritize and improve certain areas. Remember that balance is key to achieving fulfillment in all areas of your life. How to use the life energy wheel refer to the additional information section.

Seek feedback from others. The fastest way to success is to model successful people. Ask for input from people who know you well, such as family, friends, or colleagues. They may have insights that can help you identify your values.

Think about your long-term goals. What do you want to achieve in your life? What values or principles are most important to you in achieving those goals? Then, use your values as a roadmap to help you achieve your dreams.

Most importantly our values can significantly impact your personal energy in your life. When your values are aligned with your actions and decisions, it provides a sense of purpose and meaning that energizes and motivates you. On the other hand, when your actions and decisions are not in alignment with your values, it can lead to a sense of conflict or disharmony that can drain your energy.

When you are living in alignment with your values, it can provide a sense of direction and purpose in life. This can motivate and energize you, as you make choices that align with what you believe is important and meaningful. A sense of purpose and direction can give you the drive and energy to pursue your goals, tackle challenges, and overcome obstacles. Furthermore, living in alignment with your values can provide a sense of fulfillment and satisfaction, further boosting your motivation and energy levels. This sense of purpose and motivation can help to keep you going, even when faced with difficulties, and provide the foundation for a fulfilling and meaningful life.

Living in alignment with your values means making choices consistent with your beliefs, attitudes, and principles. This can increase confidence and self-esteem, as you are being true to yourself and making decisions that reflect your unique identity. When you feel confident and have a high level of self-esteem, you are more likely to take action, pursue your goals, and engage in meaningful activities. This increased level of personal energy can help you overcome challenges and obstacles, allowing you to make positive changes in your life and achieve your full potential. Additionally, when living in alignment with your values, you are likely to feel more content and satisfied, which can contribute to overall well-being and happiness.

Living in alignment with your values means making choices and taking actions consistent with what you believe is important and meaningful in life. When you are true to your values, you feel a sense of inner harmony and peace, which can lead to increased feelings of personal fulfillment. The fulfillment that comes from living in alignment with your values can be a powerful source of motivation and energy, lifting your spirits and giving you a sense of purpose and direction. This can help you achieve your goals and lead a more satisfying and fulfilling life.

Living according to your values positively impacts personal energy by providing motivation, purpose, self-confidence, and satisfaction. Raising your standards can also affect personal energy levels by providing a sense of direction, clarity, and increased motivation

Determining your values is a crucial step towards achieving a fulfilling life. Remember that your values are the foundation upon which you build your life, so take the time to reflect and identify what truly matters to you.

This reminds me a story my father told me. Once upon a time, a wise old tortoise named Tito lived in a dense forest. Tito was known for his wisdom and was respected by all the animals in the forest. Then, one day, a young deer came to him seeking guidance.

"O wise Tito, I have felt lost and uncertain about my future. I don't know what I want to do with my life. Can you help me?" asked the deer.

Tito looked at the deer and said, "Reflect on your experiences. Think about the situations in which you felt most fulfilled or satisfied. What values or principles were important to you in those moments? This can help you identify what is truly important to you."

The deer thanked Tito and left, deep in thought. He thought about all the moments in his life where he felt truly fulfilled and happy. He remembered the time when he helped a lost fox find its way back home, when he made a new friend, and when he won a race. He realized that he had acted with kindness, compassion, and perseverance in all those moments.

Excited, the deer went back to Tito and said, "O wise one, I have realized that what is truly important to me are kindness, compassion, and perseverance. I want to live my life helping others and spreading joy."

Tito nodded and said, "That's a great start, my young friend. But it would help if you also reflected on your priorities. Use the life energy wheel to identify the areas of your life that matter most to you."

The deer followed Tito's advice and used the life energy wheel to reflect on his priorities. He realized that his family, career, and health were the most important areas for him. He then set long-term goals that aligned with his values and priorities.

Finally, Tito said, "It's important to seek feedback from others. Ask your family, friends, and colleagues for their honest opinions about your strengths and weaknesses. This can help you improve and grow."

The deer followed Tito's advice and sought feedback from others. He used the feedback to improve himself and become a better version of himself.

And so, the deer went on to live a fulfilling life, helping others and spreading joy wherever he went. And Tito continued to share his wisdom with all the animals in the forest, guiding them on their journey of self-discovery.

From this story, we can learn about the importance of self-reflection and seeking guidance from others in determining our values and priorities.

This story teaches us that determining our values and priorities is an ongoing process that requires self-reflection, introspection, and feedback from others. By reflecting on our experiences, beliefs, and priorities, we can better understand ourselves and what we truly value. Likewise, by seeking feedback from others, we can gain a different perspective and insights into our blind spots.

Finally, the story highlights the importance of setting long-term goals that align with our values and priorities. By setting goals that are meaningful and aligned with our values, we can work towards living a fulfilling life consistent with our values and principles.

Know Your Value Summary

1. Reflect on your experiences: Think about the moments in your life when you felt most fulfilled, happy, and satisfied. What values were important to you in those moments? This will give you a good starting point to identify your core values.

2. Consider your beliefs: What do you believe in, and why? What are your guiding principles? This will help you to understand the values that are most important to you.

3. Reflect on your priorities: What are the most important aspects of your life? How do you allocate your time and energy towards them? Use the Life Energy Wheel to assess the balance in your life. If the wheel appears imbalanced, it means you need to prioritize and improve certain areas.

4. Seek feedback from others: Ask for input from people who know you well, such as family, friends, or colleagues. They may have insights that can help you identify your values.

5. Think about your long-term goals: What do you want to achieve in your life? What values or principles are most important to you in achieving those goals? Use your values as a roadmap to help you achieve your dreams.

6. Live in alignment with your values: Make choices and take actions that are consistent with what you believe is important and meaningful in life. When you are true to your values, you feel a sense of inner harmony and peace, and this can lead to increased feelings of personal fulfillment.

By determining your values and living in alignment with them, you can increase your personal energy and achieve a more fulfilling life. Remember that your values are the foundation upon which you build your life, so take the time to reflect and identify what truly matters to you.

Boost Your Performance with Higher Standards

To find your standards, you need to ask yourself what you really want in life. Start by thinking about what's most important to you in terms of your relationships, career, health, finances, spirituality, and any other areas that are meaningful to you.

Next, ask yourself what you're willing to tolerate in each of these areas. For example, if you're looking to improve your health, what are you willing to tolerate in terms of your diet, exercise, and self-care? If you're looking to enhance your career, what are you willing to tolerate in terms of your work environment, salary, and job responsibilities?

Once you have a clear idea of what you're willing to tolerate, you can start to identify your standards. Your standards are the minimum requirements that you set for yourself in each area of your life. These are the things that you absolutely must have in order to be happy, fulfilled, and successful.

To identify your standards, ask yourself the following questions:

What are the things that I absolutely must have in order to be happy, fulfilled, and successful in each area of my life?

What are the things that I'm not willing to compromise on in each area of my life?

What are the things that I'm willing to fight for in each area of my life?

As you answer these questions, write down your answers and use them to create a list of your standards. This list will serve as a guide for you as you make decisions about your life and work towards achieving your goals.

Once you have identified your current standards, here are several strategies to raise your standards and achieve the level of success you desire.

Change your limiting beliefs: Your current standards may be limited by your beliefs about what is possible or what you are capable of achieving. To raise your standards, you need to identify and challenge these limiting beliefs and replace them with empowering beliefs that support your new standards.

Model success: Find people who have achieved the level of success you desire and study their habits and mindset. This can help you identify new behaviors and ways of thinking that will help you raise your standards.

Set clear goals: Your standards are directly tied to the goals you set for yourself. To raise your standards, set goals that are compelling, challenging, and align with your values and vision for your life.

Take massive action: To achieve your new standards, you need to take massive action towards your goals. This means consistently taking small steps that move you closer to your desired outcome, even if it feels uncomfortable or challenging at first.

Celebrate your progress: As you take action toward your new standards, it's important to celebrate your progress along the way. This helps you stay motivated and reinforces the new behaviors and beliefs you are adopting.

By consistently applying these strategies, you can raise your standards and achieve the level of success and fulfillment you desire in all areas of your life.

Increase Your Standards Summary

1. Identify what's important: To find your standards, you need to ask yourself what you really want in life. Start by thinking about what's most important to you in terms of your relationships, career, health, finances, spirituality, and any other areas that are meaningful to you.

2. Determine your minimum requirements: Your standards are the minimum requirements that you set for yourself in each area of your life. These are the things that you absolutely must have in order to be happy, fulfilled, and successful.

3. Ask yourself key questions: To identify your standards, ask yourself questions like "What are the things that I absolutely must have in order to be happy, fulfilled, and successful in each area of my life?" or "What are the things that I'm not willing to compromise on in each area of my life?"

4. Write down your standards: Write down your answers to the questions and use them to create a list of your standards. This list will serve as a guide for you as you make decisions about your life and work towards achieving your goals.

5. Strategies to raise your standards: Change limiting beliefs, model success, set compelling goals, take massive action, and celebrate progress.

6. Challenge limiting beliefs: Your current standards may be limited by your beliefs about what is possible or what you are capable of achieving. To raise your standards, you need to identify and challenge these limiting beliefs and replace them with empowering beliefs that support your new standards.

7. Model success: Find people who have achieved the level of success you desire and study their habits and mindset. This can help you identify new behaviors and ways of thinking that will help you raise your standards.

8. Set compelling goals: Your standards are directly tied to the goals you set for yourself. To raise your standards, set goals that are compelling, challenging, and align with your values and vision for your life.

9. Take massive action: To achieve your new standards, you need to take massive action towards your goals. This means consistently taking small steps that move you closer to your desired outcome, even if it feels uncomfortable or challenging at first.

10. Celebrate progress: As you take action towards your new standards, it's important to celebrate your progress along the way. This helps you stay motivated and reinforces the new behaviors and beliefs you are adopting.

Discover How to Live in the Present Moment

Are you constantly feeling overwhelmed by the demands of modern life, always rushing from one task to the next without taking a moment to breathe? Do you find yourself glued to your phone, missing out on the beauty of the world around you? In today's fast-paced world, it's easy to get caught up in the chaos and lose sight of what's truly important. But there is a way to break free from the cycle of stress and distraction, and it starts with living in the present moment. Let me tell you the story of Rusty, a young teenage cub who learned the power of mindfulness and living in the present moment, and how his journey can inspire us all to find greater peace, joy, and fulfillment in our lives.

Once upon a time, in a lush green forest, there lived a young teenage cub named Rusty. Rusty was a bright and energetic cub, but he was always glued to his phone, scrolling through social media and playing video games.

One day, as Rusty was walking through the forest, he stumbled upon an old lion perched on a boulder. The lion noticed Rusty's preoccupation with his phone and said, "Rusty, why do you spend so much time on that little device? You're missing out on the beauty of the world around you."

Rusty was taken aback and replied, "But there's so much to see and do on my phone! I don't want to miss out on anything."

The lion smiled and said, "I understand, but there's so much more to life than what's on that screen. Look around you and notice the colors of the leaves, the smell of the flowers, and the sounds of the birds. Focus on the present moment, Rusty."

At first, Rusty was skeptical, but he decided to take the lion's advice and put down his phone. He noticed the vibrant colors of the flowers, the soft rustling of the leaves, and the sweet chirping of the birds. He realized how much he had been missing out on by being glued to his phone.

Rusty also realized that he was often multitasking and not fully present in the moment. He would try to do his homework, play video games, and chat with friends all at once. But after talking with the wise old lion, he learned the importance of doing one thing at a time and being fully present in the moment.

He also began to practice mindfulness and meditation, taking time each day to focus on his breath and clear his mind. And to disconnect from technology, Rusty made a habit of taking breaks from his phone and spending time in nature, where he could fully appreciate the beauty around him.

Over time, Rusty became more present, mindful, and focused. He found that he was able to enjoy life more fully and appreciate the little things that he had once overlooked. And he thanked the wise old lion for showing him the way to a more fulfilling life.

We can learn from Rusty's experience and strive to live in the present moment by taking steps such as practicing mindfulness, disconnecting from technology, and engaging in activities that bring us joy. By focusing on our breath and observing our surroundings, we can become more present and fully engage our senses. We can let go of worries about the past and future and cultivate gratitude for the small things in life. It's important to avoid multitasking and instead focus on one task at a time. Spending time in nature can also help us feel more grounded and connected to the present moment. By incorporating these practices into our daily lives, we can learn to appreciate and enjoy life more fully.

Present Moment Summary

1. Breathe deeply and focus on the present moment. Take deep breaths and focus on the sensation of the air entering and leaving your body. This helps ground you in the present moment.

2. Notice your surroundings. Pay attention to the sights, sounds, and smells around you. Be fully present in the moment and engage your senses.

3. Be mindful of your thoughts and emotions. Don't judge them, just observe them without reacting.

4. Let go of the past and don't worry about the future. Focus on what's happening right now.

5. Practice gratitude. Be thankful for the small things in life and appreciate what you have in the present moment.

6. Do one thing at a time. Focus on the task at hand and avoid multitasking.

7. Practice mindfulness meditation. This involves sitting quietly and focusing on your breath or a mantra to cultivate present moment awareness.

8. Disconnect from technology. Take breaks from social media, email, and other distractions to be fully present in the moment.

9. Engage in activities that bring you joy. Doing things, you love can help you be more present and enjoy the moment.

10. Spend time in nature. Being in nature can help you connect with the present moment and feel more grounded.

Uncover the Key to Staying Healthy and Fit

When it comes to feeling sluggish and needing more energy, it can be challenging to know where to turn. You may be tempted to reach for a sugary snack or a caffeine-laden drink to try and perk yourself up, but these quick fixes often come with a crash later on. That's where exercise comes in. Regular physical activity has been proven time and time again to be an effective way to boost your energy levels naturally.

As someone always looking for ways to enhance performance, I can attest to the power of exercise. Whether you're hitting the gym, running, or taking a yoga class, moving your body can do wonders for your energy levels. In addition to the physical benefits, exercise can also improve your mental and emotional well-being. For example, studies have shown that regular exercise can reduce symptoms of anxiety and depression and improve overall mood.

Throughout this chapter, we will explore the various ways in which exercise can boost your energy levels. From improving circulation to increasing endorphins, we'll cover it all. We'll also provide practical tips on incorporating physical activity into your daily routine, no matter how busy you are. Whether you're a seasoned athlete or a beginner looking to start your fitness journey, this chapter has something for everyone. So, get ready to feel energized and motivated as we explore the power of exercise.

One of the main ways that exercise boosts energy levels is by improving circulation throughout the body. When you exercise, your heart pumps more blood to your muscles, delivering oxygen and nutrients more efficiently. This increased circulation can lead to greater endurance, allowing you to sustain physical activity for longer periods without feeling tired or fatigued.

Another way that exercise can boost energy levels is by increasing endorphins. Endorphins are the body's natural feel-good chemicals released in response to physical activity. These natural chemicals can create feelings of euphoria, commonly called the "runner's high." The release of endorphins can also reduce feelings of stress and anxiety, improving overall mood and motivation. Endorphins can provide a natural energy boost, helping to reduce the likelihood of feeling fatigued by reducing negative emotions. In this way, exercise can improve energy levels and a greater sense of well-being.

Exercise not only increases the production of endorphins but can also boost the production of other hormones and neurotransmitters that contribute to improved energy levels and overall well-being. For example, exercise can increase the production of dopamine, a neurotransmitter that plays a key role in motivation, pleasure, and reward. Higher dopamine levels can enhance overall well-being, provide a sense of accomplishment and satisfaction, and improve energy levels.

Another neurotransmitter that can be affected by exercise is serotonin. Exercise can increase the production of serotonin, which is responsible for regulating mood, appetite, and sleep. Higher serotonin levels can reduce feelings of depression, anxiety, and stress, leading to increased energy levels and a better sense of overall well-being.

Exercise can also boost testosterone levels in both men and women. Testosterone is a hormone that promotes muscle growth, bone density, and libido, leading to improved physical fitness, increased energy levels, and overall well-being.

Additionally, exercise can increase growth hormone production, essential for maintaining healthy body composition, building muscle mass, and repairing tissue. Higher growth hormone levels can improve overall energy levels and promote faster recovery after exercise.

In addition to these hormones and chemicals, exercise can improve insulin sensitivity, regulate blood sugar levels, and reduce inflammation, all of which can contribute to higher energy levels and overall health. By incorporating regular physical activity into your routine, you can take advantage of all these benefits and enjoy a healthier, more energized life.

Exercise can also improve the quality of your sleep. Regular physical activity can help regulate your body's internal clock, making it easier to fall asleep at night and wake up refreshed in the morning. By getting more restful sleep, you'll have more energy to tackle your day and accomplish your goals.

So, how can you incorporate exercise into your daily routine? It doesn't have to be complicated or time-consuming. Even small changes can make a big difference. For example, take a walk during your lunch break or do a quick yoga session before bed. Also, consider joining a fitness class or finding a workout buddy to help keep you motivated.

The key is finding an activity you enjoy and can realistically fit into your schedule. Then, by making exercise a regular part of your routine, you'll reap the benefits of improved energy levels and overall well-being. So, what are you waiting for? Get moving and feel the power of exercise!

It's important to note that consistency is key when it comes to exercise. It's better to start with a small amount of exercise and gradually increase it over time rather than trying too much too soon and risking injury or burnout. Aim for at least 30 minutes of moderate-intensity exercise most days of the week. This could include brisk walking, cycling, swimming, or strength training.

If you need help figuring out where to start, consider working with a personal trainer or fitness professional. They can help you create a safe and effective exercise program tailored to your needs and goals. They can also guide proper form and technique, which can help prevent injury and improve results.

Remember, exercise doesn't have to be a chore. There are many different types of physical activity to choose from, so find something that you enjoy and makes you feel good. Whether it's dancing, hiking, or playing a sport, there's an activity for everyone.

When you need an energy boost, it's easy to reach for a caffeinated drink or a sugary snack. However, these quick fixes can lead to a crash and leave you feeling more sluggish than before. Instead, consider incorporating physical activity into your routine for a natural energy boost. For example, taking a quick walk, doing a set of push-ups, jumping jacks, or air squats can help increase blood flow, oxygenation, and the release of endorphins, dopamine, serotonin, and other hormones and neurotransmitters that can improve your energy levels and overall well-being. These simple exercises can be done almost anywhere and anytime, making incorporating them into your daily routine easy. You can experience sustained energy levels and better overall health by choosing physical activity over quick fixes.

Finally, exercise is a powerful way to boost your energy levels naturally. It can improve circulation, increase endorphins, and improve the quality of your sleep, all of which contribute to greater motivation and a better sense of vitality. By establishing healthy habits, such as getting enough sleep, eating a balanced diet, and making exercise a regular part of your routine, you can improve your energy levels and maintain good health. On the other hand, unhealthy habits like smoking, excessive alcohol consumption, and a sedentary lifestyle can have the opposite effect, leading to fatigue and a lack of energy. Therefore, it's important to prioritize healthy habits and make physical activity a regular part of your daily routine. So, why not put on your sneakers and take a walk or try a quick workout today? By doing so, you'll be taking a step towards a healthier and more energized life.

Exercise Can Boost Your Energy Levels Summary

1. Improves circulation - Exercise increases blood flow throughout the body, which helps to deliver oxygen and nutrients to your muscles and organs. This increased circulation can help you feel more alert and energized.

2. Releases endorphins - Exercise stimulates the release of endorphins, which are natural chemicals that can improve your mood and reduce feelings of stress and anxiety. This can provide a natural energy boost and help you feel more motivated.

3. Enhances sleep quality - Regular exercise can improve the quality of your sleep, leading to more restful and rejuvenating rest. This can help you feel more refreshed and energized during the day.

4. Increases dopamine and serotonin - Exercise increases the production of dopamine and serotonin, two neurotransmitters that play a role in mood regulation. Higher levels of these chemicals can enhance overall feelings of well-being and provide a sense of accomplishment and satisfaction.

5. Boosts testosterone and growth hormone - Exercise can increase testosterone levels in both men and women, leading to improved physical fitness, increased energy levels, and overall well-being. Exercise also increases the production of growth hormone, which is essential for maintaining healthy body composition, building muscle mass, and repairing tissue.

6. Improves insulin sensitivity - Exercise can improve insulin sensitivity, which can help regulate blood sugar levels and reduce the likelihood of feeling fatigued.

7. Reduces inflammation - Exercise can help reduce inflammation in the body, which can contribute to higher energy levels and overall health.

By incorporating regular exercise into your routine, you can enjoy all of these benefits and experience a greater sense of vitality and energy in your daily life.

Power of Positive Thinking

Do you ever find yourself feeling sluggish or drained? Maybe you wake up in the morning feeling like you can't muster the energy to tackle the day ahead. If you're looking for a way to increase your energy and feel more motivated, there's one powerful tool you can use: positive thinking.

Positive thinking and attitudes are often underestimated, but they can truly transform your life. By focusing on the positive aspects of your life, you can experience more joy, happiness, fulfillment, and energy. Positive thinking can also help you build stronger relationships, increase confidence, and improve overall well-being.

The truth is, positive thinking is not just a nice-to-have; it's a must-have. When you focus on the positive aspects of your life, you open yourself up to a world of possibilities. You start to see opportunities that you might have missed before, and you begin to feel more motivated and energized. This positive mindset is contagious, and it can spread to every aspect of your life.

Positive thinking doesn't mean ignoring the challenges and difficulties in your life. Instead, it means choosing to focus on the positive aspects of those challenges and finding solutions instead of dwelling on the negative. When you dwell on negativity, you create a vicious cycle leading to anxiety, depression, and other mental health challenges. When you approach problems with a positive mindset, you're more likely to find creative solutions and come out on top.

One strategy for cultivating positive thinking is to practice gratitude. Take a few moments each day to reflect on what you're thankful for, whether it's your family, your health, or the opportunities you've been given. This can help you shift your focus away from negative thoughts and toward the good in your life.

Surrounding yourself with positive influences is a powerful strategy to cultivate positivity. When you spend time with individuals who possess a positive outlook on life, you tend to embrace that same mindset. In addition, being aware of the information you consume is crucial, so choose to read uplifting books and articles and listen to music or podcasts that inspire you. Immersing yourself in positivity will naturally help you adopt a more positive mindset.

In addition, seeking friends, mentors, or colleagues who uplift and inspire you is essential. Being around people who are encouraging and support you can significantly impact your energy levels and overall well-being. When you surround yourself with positive influences, you're more likely to see the good in situations and approach challenges positively.

Remember, the people you surround yourself with can drain your energy or fuel your spirit. So choose your company wisely and invest in relationships that uplift and empower you. Surrounding yourself with positivity will help you stay motivated, energized, and focused on achieving your goals.

Lastly, taking care of your physical health is crucial to cultivating positivity. Exercise regularly, eat a healthy diet, and get plenty of rest. When your body feels good, your mind will follow suit, and you'll have the energy and motivation to maintain a positive outlook.

Finally, remember that positive thinking is a practice, not a destination. It's something you need to work on every day. When you find yourself slipping into negative thoughts, take a moment to pause and reframe your thinking. Ask yourself, "What's one positive thing I can focus on right now?" This simple shift can help you increase your energy and feel more motivated.

The power of positive thinking is real, and it can profoundly impact your energy levels and overall well-being. By practicing gratitude, surrounding yourself with positive people, and making positivity a daily practice, you can cultivate a positive mindset and unlock your full potential. So, start today and see the amazing benefits for yourself!

Power of Positive Thinking Summary

1. Your mindset has a profound impact on your energy levels and overall well-being.

2. By focusing on the positive aspects of your life, you can experience more joy, happiness, and fulfillment.

3. Positive thinking can help you build stronger relationships, increase your confidence, and find solutions to challenges.

4. Practicing gratitude is a powerful strategy for cultivating positivity and shifting your focus away from negativity.

5. Surrounding yourself with positive influences, such as uplifting books, music, and people, can help you adopt a positive mindset.

6. Investing in relationships that uplift and empower you can significantly impact your energy levels and overall well-being.

7. Taking care of your physical health is crucial to cultivating positivity, such as exercise, healthy diet, and plenty of rest.

8. Positive thinking is a practice, not a destination, and requires daily effort to maintain.

9. By cultivating a positive mindset, you can unlock your full potential and experience the amazing benefits of positive thinking.

Realize the Power of Surrendering: Letting Go

Are you feeling stressed and anxious because you're trying to control things outside your control? Well, I've got some tips for you on how to let go of this need and find inner peace.

First, it's important to recognize when you're trying to control something. This awareness is the first step to letting go. Next, ask yourself if it's within your power to control the situation or person. If not, remind yourself that it's okay to let go.

Secondly, practice mindfulness. Focus on the present moment and let go of trying to control the future. Remember, the future is uncertain, and worrying about it won't change anything.

Thirdly, it's important to let go of the pursuit of perfection. Numerous successful individuals have acknowledged that perfectionism can have detrimental effects on our mental health and productivity, leading to procrastination, fear of failure, and burnout. Therefore, rather than striving for perfection, focusing on progress and improvement is more beneficial.

As an engineer, I had to confront my struggles with perfectionism and acknowledge how it negatively impacted my life. I used to hold up load deliveries until they met my standards, attempting to fix everything at once. However, I learned that "done" is better than "perfect" and that any issues could be addressed in subsequent load deliveries.

Moreover, I realized that striving for perfectionism can foster unrealistic expectations, causing me to be overly critical of myself and others. It also led to procrastination and a fear of failure, as I hesitated to take action or try new things in case, they didn't meet my high standards. This behavior contributed to burnout and affected my mental health.

Additionally, my perfectionism fed into the "nice guy" syndrome, where I believed that being accommodating and agreeable would lead to love and affection. As a result, I put the needs of others before my own and became resentful when my efforts were not reciprocated. I thought that if I were perfect, I would be accepted and loved, causing me to overlook my own needs and boundaries, ultimately leading to disappointment and frustration.

Perfectionism also resulted in overcompensation for believing I was not good enough. I set high standards for myself and others, constantly attempting to prove my worth or value. This led to overworking, being overly critical of myself and others, or seeking validation from others. In addition, negative self-talk and low self-esteem reinforced the belief that I was not good enough, creating a self-defeating cycle.

To overcome perfectionism, I first recognized that these behaviors were not serving me well. Next, I reflected on my actions and behavior, identifying patterns of perfectionism. Then, I established boundaries by communicating healthy boundaries with others, stating what I would and would not tolerate in relationships, and standing up for myself when those boundaries were violated. I stopped seeking validation from others and focused on building self-worth and self-esteem. I learned to say no and stopped feeling guilty for not doing things I didn't want. I prioritized my needs and wants and stopped sacrificing my happiness for the sake of others. Breaking old habits took time and effort, but with patience and the right approach, I overcame perfectionism and built healthier and more authentic relationships. Seeking professional help from a therapist or counselor may be beneficial to develop coping strategies and work through underlying issues.

Fourthly, it's important to seek support when letting go of the need to control. You can talk to a trusted friend or therapist about your desire to control things and work on letting go together. Don't be afraid to ask for help; sometimes, it's okay to need assistance.

Finally, practicing relaxation techniques such as deep breathing, meditation, or yoga can help let go of the need to control and find inner peace. One such technique is box breathing, square breathing, or four-square breathing. This technique involves inhaling for a count of four, holding the breath for a count of four, exhaling for a count of four, and holding the breath again for a count of four. Repeating this process for several cycles allows you to focus on your breath and clear your mind.

Box breathing is a powerful technique to help manage stress and improve mental and physical well-being. The Navy SEALs have used it to remain calm in high-stress situations, and can also be used to increase energy levels when needed. The technique is easy to learn and can be practiced anywhere, anytime, making it a valuable tool for managing stress and improving overall well-being.

Remember that letting go of the need to control external factors takes time and effort. Be kind to yourself and focus on what you can control, such as your thoughts and actions. You can unlock a happier life by appreciating what you already have and focusing on the present moment.

Letting Go Summary

1. Recognize when you are trying to control something that is outside of your control.

2. Practice mindfulness by bringing your attention to the present moment and letting go of trying to control the future.

3. Let go of the pursuit of perfection and focus on progress and improvement.

4. Seek support when letting go of the need to control. Talk to a trusted friend or therapist about your desire to control things and work on letting go together.

5. Practice relaxation techniques such as deep breathing, meditation, or yoga, and consider learning the box breathing technique.

6. Establish healthy boundaries with others, prioritize your own needs and wants, and stop seeking validation from others.

7. Be kind to yourself and focus on what you can control, such as your thoughts and actions. Remember that letting go of the need to control external factors takes time and effort.

Unlock a Happier Life
By Appreciating What You Have

Practicing gratitude and focusing on the positive aspects of your life is essential for improving your mental health and overall well-being. In this post, we will delve into two powerful techniques that can help you cultivate an attitude of gratitude: keeping a gratitude journal and sharing your appreciation with others.

Keeping a gratitude journal is an effective way to shift your mindset and focus on the positive. Every evening, take a few minutes to write down three things you are grateful for and reflect on how those things have impacted your life. Doing so lets you train your brain to look for the good in every situation. Additionally, make it a point to express gratitude to someone else daily. This could be through a heartfelt message, a small gift, or a simple compliment.

Gratitude is not just about saying thank you, but also taking action to show your appreciation. Doing something kind for someone else daily can spread positivity and make a meaningful impact in someone's life. It could be as simple as holding the door open for someone or offering to help a co-worker with a task.

Gratitude is about finding the positive in every situation, even during the most challenging times. Take time each day to reflect on the lessons you have learned from your struggles and find something to be grateful for in each situation. By doing so, you can grow and learn from your experiences.

Sharing your gratitude with others is a powerful way to connect with the universe and attract positivity. Expressing gratitude for the people in your life who have helped you along the way is just as important as being grateful for the things you have. Take time each day to thank someone instrumental in your journey, whether a mentor, colleague, or loved one.

Practicing gratitude and focusing on the positive aspects of your life can have a transformative impact on your well-being. Keeping a gratitude journal and sharing your gratitude with others are two powerful techniques that can help shift your mindset towards positivity. Whether you write down your gratitude or express it out loud, focusing on what you are grateful for can help improve your outlook on life. So, take some time today to reflect on all the things you are thankful for and share that gratitude with the people in your life. Your positivity and gratitude will benefit you and those around you.

Cultivating an attitude of gratitude requires dedication and patience, but with consistent practice, you can enhance your overall well-being. Let go of negativity and surround yourself with uplifting people who will boost your energy. Focus on what you have rather than what you lack and appreciate the small things in life. Doing so will attract more positivity into your life and create a happier, more fulfilling existence.

Gratitude Summary

1. Start keeping a gratitude journal - every evening, write down three things you are grateful for and reflect on how those things have impacted your life.

2. Take action to show your appreciation - every day, do something kind for someone else, whether it's sending a thoughtful message, buying someone a coffee, or giving them a compliment.

3. Find the positive in challenging situations - take time each day to reflect on the lessons you have learned from your struggles and find something to be grateful for in each of those situations.

4. Share your gratitude with others - take time each day to express gratitude for the people in your life who have helped you along the way, whether it's a mentor, colleague, or loved one.

By following these action items, you can cultivate an attitude of gratitude and improve your well-being. Remember to take some time each day to reflect on all the things you are grateful for and share your gratitude with those around you.

Say Goodbye to Negativity:
Attracting Uplifting People Now

Have you ever been around someone who was always negative or had nothing positive to say. These people zap your energy, and provide no value to you what so ever.

I want to talk to you about the importance of surrounding yourself with positive, supportive people. This is something that has been emphasized by some of the most successful and influential people in the world, that I follow on YouTube. All of them have one thing in common: choosing the wrong people to surround yourself with can have a huge impact on your mental health, overall well-being, and energy.

First and foremost, surrounding yourself with positive, supportive people can help you maintain a positive attitude and outlook on life. As Ed Mylett often says, "Your attitude is your altitude." In other words, how you think and feel about yourself and your life can either hold you back or propel you forward. If you surround yourself with people who are negative, critical, or unsupportive, it can be incredibly draining and demotivating. On the other hand, if you surround yourself with positive, encouraging, and uplifting people, it can help you stay motivated and inspired to pursue your goals and dreams.

Being around positive, supportive people can also help you build your self-esteem and confidence. As Tony Robbins says, "The quality of your life is directly proportional to the quality of the relationships in your life." So when you have people around you who believe in you, support you, and encourage you to be your best self, it can help you feel more confident in your abilities and more willing to take risks and try new things.

But most importantly, surrounding yourself with positive, supportive people can help you take care of your mental health and overall well-being. As Tim Grover says, "Your environment has a huge impact on your results." Surrounding yourself with people who prioritize self-care, mental health, and well-being can help you do the same. You can learn from their habits and behaviors, and they can hold you accountable for taking care of yourself.

Of course, it's important to note that not everyone in your life will always be positive and supportive. We all have our off days, and we all have moments of negativity or criticism. But as David Goggins says, "You are the average of the five people you spend the most time with." So, it's important to be mindful of who those five people are and how they impact your life. If someone in your life is consistently negative or unsupportive, it may be time to reassess that relationship and determine whether it's healthy for you to continue.

If you find yourself lacking good supporting people in your life, start seeking out new connections by joining a club or groups that aligns with your interests and values, and make an effort to meet new people who are positive and supportive.

Remember it's a two-way street you must also be giving value to others to get value back so it is important to practice good communication skills. Be open and honest with the people you are close with, and make an effort to listen actively and show empathy. This can help strengthen your relationships and create a positive and supportive environment.

In conclusion, surrounding yourself with positive, supportive people can greatly impact your mental health, overall well-being, and energy. As Dr. Wayne Dyer says, "Surround yourself with those who see greatness within you, even when you don't see it in yourself." When you have people around you who believe in you, support you, and encourage you to be your best self, it can help you achieve more than you ever thought possible. So, take time to assess the people in your life and determine whether they're helping or holding you back. And remember, as Bedros Keuilian says, "You become who you surround yourself with." Choose wisely!

Surround Yourself with Positive People Summary

1. Evaluate the people in your life and assess whether they are positive and supportive.

2. If you find that someone in your life is consistently negative or unsupportive, consider whether it's healthy for you to continue that relationship.

3. Seek out new connections by joining a club or group that aligns with your interests and values, and make an effort to meet new people who are positive and supportive.

4. Practice good communication skills by being open and honest with the people you are close with, and make an effort to listen actively and show empathy.

5. Be mindful of the kind of energy you bring to your relationships and strive to be a positive and supportive influence on those around you.

Uncover Freedom from Self-Imposed Obstacles

We are not born with limited beliefs; we learn them as we get older these limited beliefs are negative thoughts and ideas that we hold about ourselves or the world that limit our potential and ability to achieve our goals. These beliefs may be self-imposed or may be influenced by others, and they can hold you back by causing you to doubt your abilities, potential, or worth. Examples of limited beliefs include:

- *"I'm not smart enough."*
- *"I'm not good enough."*
- *"I'm not talented enough."*
- *"I'm not attractive enough."*
- *"I'm not tall enough."*
- *"I'm not worthy of love or respect."*
- *"I can't achieve my goals."*
- *"I'm not capable of change."*

There are countless negative beliefs that can hold us back, but when we refuse to give them power, we'll unlock a sense of freedom.

I spent over ten thousand hours and over one hundred thousand dollars reprogramming my mind to eliminate my self-imposed obstacles preventing me from truly living my life. To be truthful, it's an ongoing battle in my mind I fight every day. It's a battle worth fighting because it's your life on the line. When you look back at your life when the time is up, you can hold your head high that you lived a fulfilled life. A life lived with no regrets. My father told me on his deathbed that he does not want to have any regrets going into the afterlife. If you do or don't believe in heaven, it doesn't matter. What matters is you are here right now, living the life given to you.

One thing captivating regarding life is we all have different journeys and outcomes that are unique to all of us. Also, we have different time schedules for that discovery of freedom. Remember that limited beliefs can be deeply ingrained and difficult to change, but it is possible to overcome them. In the meantime, enjoy the journey and be open to whatever happens in life.

I want to share some strategies with you for eliminating limiting beliefs and ways to transform them.

To start eliminating limited beliefs, you must first identify them. A limited belief is a belief that you hold about yourself or the world that is holding you back. For example, you might believe that you need to be more intelligent to succeed in your dream career or that you need to be more worthy of love and happiness. These beliefs are often deeply ingrained and hard to identify, but they are the key to unlocking your potential.

Next, challenge your limited belief by asking yourself, "Is this belief true?" Often, our limited beliefs are based on assumptions or past experiences that are no longer relevant. For example, if you believe you're not smart enough to succeed in your dream career, challenge that belief by questioning whether you've given it your all. Have you taken the necessary steps to learn and grow in your chosen field? Have you sought out mentorship or coaching?

Replace the belief with a new, empowering belief. This belief should be based on evidence and truth and support your goals and aspirations. For example, if you previously believed you were not smart enough to succeed in your dream career, replace that belief with the belief that you can learn and grow in your chosen field with hard work and dedication.

To reinforce your new belief, visualize yourself succeeding in your goals. Imagine yourself achieving your dreams and feeling the sense of accomplishment that comes with it. This visualization will help to rewire your brain and reinforce your new, empowering belief.

To truly reinforce your new belief, you need to take action. First, set goals and take steps toward achieving them. Then, celebrate your small wins and use them to prove your new belief is true.

Eliminating limited beliefs is hard work, and being kind to yourself is crucial. One way to cultivate self-compassion is to recognize your progress and extend patience toward yourself. Remember that change takes time and that setbacks are a natural part of the process.

Finally, consider seeking coaching or mentorship if you need help to eliminate a limited belief. A coach can help you identify your limiting beliefs and provide the tools and support to eliminate them and achieve your goals.

In summary, eliminating limited beliefs is essential for unlocking your full potential. By identifying your limited belief, challenging it, replacing it with a new, empowering belief, visualizing success, taking action, practicing self-compassion, and seeking coaching, you can overcome any obstacle and achieve your wildest dreams. Remember, as Tony Robbins says, "Beliefs have the power to create and the power to destroy. Human beings can take any experience of their lives and create a meaning that disempowers them or can literally save their lives." So, choose your beliefs wisely and watch your life transform.

It's important to note that this process is highly individualized and may look different for each person, depending on their limiting beliefs and goals. Additionally, coaches and therapists often use various techniques and tools to help their clients eliminate their limiting beliefs, such as emotional release techniques and reframing negative experiences.

Eliminate Limited Beliefs Steps Summary

Step 1: Identify Your Limited Belief

Step 2: Challenge Your Limited Belief

Step 3: Replace the Belief

Step 4: Visualize Success

Step 5: Take Action to Reinforce New Belief

Step 6: Practice Self-Compassion

Step 7: Seek Coaching

Say Goodbye to Stress - Here's How!

Are you feeling stressed out and overwhelmed? If so, you're not alone. Stress is a common experience that affects many of us. But the good news is that there are tools and techniques that we can use to reduce stress and bring more calmness and joy into our lives. Today, we're going to explore some powerful strategies for managing stress.

First, let's start by identifying the sources of our stress. Sometimes, we may not even realize what is causing us to feel stressed. Is it work-related? Family-related? Money-related? By identifying the source of our stress, we can take steps to address it directly. For example, if you're feeling stressed because of work, you could talk to your boss about your workload or seek support from a co-worker.

Next, let's make time for relaxation. It's essential to take breaks from the hustle and bustle of everyday life and do something that you enjoy. This could be anything from reading a book to taking a bath to listen to music. Whatever it is, make sure it's something that brings you joy and helps you to relax.

Incorporating exercise into your daily routine is another powerful tool for reducing stress. Exercise releases endorphins that promote feelings of happiness and well-being. It's also an excellent way to release tension in the body. You don't need to do a full-on workout to experience the benefits of exercise. A brisk walk or some light yoga can be just as effective.

Getting enough sleep is also crucial for managing stress. Lack of sleep can lead to increased anxiety and irritability, making it harder to cope with stress. Aim to get 7-8 hours of sleep each night and establish a consistent sleep routine to help your body and mind; relax and rejuvenate.

Deep breathing, meditation, and yoga are also effective tools for reducing stress. These practices help us to focus on the present moment and slow down our minds. Try practicing deep breathing for a few minutes each day or meditating for 10-15 minutes in the morning or evening.

Stress is a natural part of life, but it doesn't have to control us. By identifying the sources of our stress, making time for relaxation, exercising regularly, getting enough sleep, and practicing deep breathing, meditation, and yoga, we can reduce stress and experience more joy and calmness.

Remember, stress is not a permanent state and can be managed. So, let's say goodbye to stress and hello to a more peaceful, happy life!

Goodbye To Stress Summary

1. Practice Mindfulness: Mindfulness is the act of being present and fully engaged in the moment. It can help you manage stress by reducing anxiety and promoting relaxation. You can practice mindfulness by meditating, doing yoga, or simply taking a few deep breaths when you feel stressed.

2. Get Enough Sleep: Lack of sleep can cause stress levels to skyrocket. Make sure you're getting enough sleep each night to help reduce stress and promote overall health.

3. Exercise Regularly: Exercise is a great way to reduce stress and improve your mood. Even a short walk or a quick workout can help release endorphins, which are natural stress-fighters.

4. Connect with Others: Spending time with friends and loved ones can help reduce stress and promote a sense of well-being. Talking to someone about your problems can also help put things into perspective.

5. Take Breaks: If you're feeling overwhelmed, taking a break can be incredibly helpful. Whether it's a quick walk around the block or a weekend getaway, taking time to recharge can help you manage stress and feel refreshed.

The Path to True Happiness
Is Detaching From Outcome

I've come to understand a fundamental truth about true happiness that took me many years to realize. It's not about achieving a particular outcome or result but rather the journey we take to get there. When I was younger, I believed success and happiness were directly tied to achieving specific goals. So, for example, if I could get that car, I would finally win over the girl of my dreams, and my life would be complete. Or, if I could win a competition, I would eventually gain the admiration and envy of others, thus proving my worth. And if I could earn a college degree, I would finally show all those doubters who said I would never amount to anything.

However, as I've grown older and experienced more of life's challenges and triumphs, I've realized that it's not the outcome that truly matters. Instead, it's the process of working towards that goal, overcoming obstacles, and learning and growing along the way that brings true happiness. Looking back on my life, I don't remember the awards or the trophies I've received, but rather the struggles and triumphs that led me to them. The stories and memories stick with me, not the material possessions or achievements.

True happiness is found in the journey, not the destination. It's in the process of overcoming challenges, growing, and learning from our experiences. So, as you go through life, remember to enjoy the ride and appreciate the journey, for that is where true happiness lies.

The remedy lies in detaching oneself from the outcome. This entails releasing our attachment to a particular result and concentrating on the process. Furthermore, it implies discovering happiness and satisfaction in the process, irrespective of the outcome.

Here are some ways you can detach from the outcome and find true happiness:

Focus on the process. Instead of obsessing over the outcome, focus on the process of achieving your goals. Enjoy the journey, and find joy in the small victories.

Let go of expectations. We set ourselves up for disappointment when we have rigid expectations about how things should turn out. Instead, approach each situation with an open mind and a willingness to learn.

Practice gratitude. Gratitude is a powerful tool for finding happiness in the present moment. Take time each day to reflect on what you are grateful for, and appreciate the good things in your life.

Embrace failure. Failure is not the opposite of success; it's part of the process. When we detach from the outcome, we can embrace failure as a learning opportunity and grow from our mistakes.

Find joy in the journey. Detaching from the outcome means finding joy in achieving our goals rather than focusing solely on the result. Take time to appreciate the small moments of joy and fulfillment.

Be open to change: When too attached to a particular outcome, we may resist change or new opportunities. However, we can allow for new experiences and growth by embracing change.

Practice mindfulness: We can let go of our attachment to the future and fully experience the journey by being present in the moment.

Set clear intentions: By focusing on our intentions rather than specific outcomes, we can stay grounded and flexible throughout the journey.

Seek support: By surrounding ourselves with supportive people who encourage and inspire us, we can reduce the pressure of achieving a particular outcome and focus on the journey.

Now, let's apply these practices to some examples from different areas of life:

In sports, if a team focuses too much on winning a particular game or championship, they may miss out on the opportunities for growth and learning that come from practicing and playing together. By reducing attachment to the outcome, they can focus on improving their skills and enjoying the journey of playing as a team.

In relationships, if we become too attached to a particular outcome, such as marriage or children, we may miss out on the joy and growth that comes from being present. Instead, we can focus on building a strong and fulfilling connection with our partner by reducing attachment to the outcome.

In business, if we become too attached to achieving a particular goal, we may take advantage of the opportunities that arise from being open to change and new experiences. By reducing attachment to the outcome, we can focus on building a strong and sustainable business that can adapt to changing circumstances.

In terms of health, if we become too attached to achieving a specific outcome, such as a particular weight or fitness level, we may miss out on the joy and growth of living a healthy lifestyle. By reducing attachment to the outcome, we can focus on building healthy habits and enjoying the journey of becoming our best selves.

Remember that success and happiness are about achieving a particular outcome and enjoying growth and self-discovery. So, let go of attachment to outcomes and embrace the beauty of the journey. You will find that it is in the journey that true happiness and fulfillment are found.

Detach from Outcome to find True Happiness Summary

1. Focus on the journey, not just the destination. Don't get so caught up in the end result that you forget to enjoy the process of getting there.

2. Practice mindfulness and living in the present moment. When you're focused on the present, you're less likely to worry about the future or get caught up in the outcome.

3. Set goals and intentions, but remain flexible in your approach. Don't become too attached to a specific outcome or way of achieving your goals.

4. Embrace uncertainty and change. Life is unpredictable, and things don't always go as planned. Learn to adapt and find joy in the unexpected.

5. Let go of perfectionism and the need for control. Trying to control every aspect of your life and outcomes can lead to stress and anxiety. Accept that some things are outside of your control and learn to let go.

6. Practice gratitude and focus on what you have, not what you lack. Appreciate the small moments of joy and beauty in your life, and let them bring you happiness.

7. Cultivate meaningful relationships and connections. True happiness often comes from the love and support of those around us.

8. Take care of your physical and mental health. A healthy body and mind can lead to a greater sense of well-being and happiness.

9. Find purpose and meaning in your life. Whether it's through work, hobbies, or volunteering, find something that brings you a sense of purpose and fulfillment.

10. Lastly, remember that happiness is a journey, not a destination. It's a daily practice that requires patience, self-reflection, and a willingness to let go of expectations and attachments.

Silencing Your Ego: The Keys to Inner Peace

In my experience as an athlete, engineer, high-performance coach, entrepreneur, and author, I have observed how our ego can hinder us from attaining genuine inner peace and success. Our ego is that inner voice that persistently tells us that we are inadequate, we need to prove ourselves, and we should always be at the forefront. It can also make us believe that we are better than others, don't need anyone's assistance, and are invincible. Although this might give us temporary satisfaction, it can lead to problems such as burnout, relationship issues, and a complete lack of inner peace. Therefore, we must quiet our ego and adopt humility to live a truly fulfilling life.

First, let's define what ego is. Ego is our sense of self, identity, and perception of who we are. It's the part of us that wants to be seen, heard, and recognized. Our ego is not inherently good or bad, but it can positively and negatively affect our lives.

On the positive side, our ego can be a source of motivation, confidence, and self-esteem. It's what drives us to achieve our goals, take risks, and succeed. In addition, our ego can help us believe in ourselves and our abilities, which is essential in any aspect of life, whether business, relationships, or personal development.

However, on the negative side, our ego can also be a source of fear, insecurity, and doubt. It's what drives us to seek validation from others, to compare ourselves to others, and to judge ourselves harshly. As a result, our ego can create a false sense of superiority, making us feel like we're better than others and causing us to push people away. It can also prevent us from learning and growing, as we resist feedback and new ideas.

To silence your ego, you must first recognize when it's trying to take control. This requires mindfulness, which is the practice of being present in the moment and fully aware of your thoughts and emotions. Mindful, you can observe your ego without getting caught up in its drama. You can recognize when your ego is trying to take control and choose to let it go.

Another key to silencing your ego is to embrace humility. Humility is the opposite of ego. It's about recognizing your limitations, acknowledging your mistakes, and accepting that you don't have all the answers. When you embrace humility, you open yourself up to learning and growth. You become more receptive to feedback, willing to take risks, and open to new ideas. In addition, humility allows you to connect with others on a deeper level and build stronger relationships.

For example, as athletes, we must acknowledge our strengths and weaknesses, recognize when to make adjustments, and be open to learning from coaches and teammates. As an entrepreneur, we need to be receptive to feedback from customers, investors, and partners, and be willing to pivot our business strategy when necessary. Finally, as high-performance coaches, we must be humble enough to admit that we don't have all the answers and be open to learning from our clients.

Silencing your ego is essential for achieving true inner peace and success. Recognize when your ego is trying to take control, practice mindfulness, and embrace humility. Remember that your ego is not inherently good or bad, but it can positively and negatively affect your life. Use your ego as a source of motivation and confidence, but also recognize when it's causing fear and insecurity. By silencing your ego, you can achieve greater happiness, fulfillment, and success than you ever thought possible.

Silencing Your Ego Summary

1. Practice mindfulness: Mindfulness meditation can help you become more aware of your thoughts and emotions, which can help you recognize when your ego is taking over. By focusing on the present moment and observing your thoughts without judgment, you can develop a greater sense of self-awareness and control.

2. Practice empathy: Try to put yourself in other people's shoes and see things from their perspective. This can help you recognize that your own perspective is not the only one and can help you become more humble and understanding.

3. Learn to accept criticism: Criticism can be hard to hear, especially when it challenges our beliefs or actions. But accepting criticism with an open mind can help you learn and grow, and it can also help you recognize that you are not always right.

4. Practice gratitude: Focusing on what you are grateful for can help you shift your focus away from your ego and toward the positive things in your

life. This can help you develop a greater sense of humility and appreciation for the people and things around you.

5. Practice self-reflection: Take time to reflect on your thoughts and actions and how they align with your values and goals. This can help you recognize when your ego is getting in the way and can help you make adjustments to better align with your true self.

Letting Go of Unrealistic Expectations

Are you feeling overwhelmed, stressed, and frustrated with the way things are going in your life? Do you constantly strive for perfection, only to end up disappointed when you fall short? If so, let go of some of your unrealistic expectations and focus on setting healthy ones instead.

Let me tell you something, my friend: holding onto unrealistic expectations is like carrying a heavy weight on your shoulders. It can weigh you down, drain your energy, and hold you back from achieving your true potential. The good news is that you can experience a newfound sense of freedom and unlock your full potential by letting go of these expectations.

So, what are healthy expectations, you ask? Healthy expectations are realistic, achievable, and aligned with your values and priorities. They are goals that challenge you without overwhelming you and inspire you to grow and improve.

For example, let's say you want to improve your physical fitness. An unrealistic expectation might be to lose 20 pounds in a month or run a marathon next week, even though you've only run a mile. On the other hand, a healthy expectation might be to commit to working out three times a week and gradually increasing your distance or intensity over time.

Another example of unrealistic expectations could be setting your sights on becoming a millionaire overnight or achieving overnight success in your business. A healthy expectation in this case would be to work hard and steadily towards your goals, focusing on building a solid foundation for your business, making incremental improvements along the way, and keeping an eye on the long-term vision.

Letting go of unrealistic expectations is not always easy. It requires a shift in mindset and a willingness to let go of perfectionism and control. It also requires a willingness to embrace failure and setbacks as opportunities for growth and learning.

But, when you let go of these expectations, you will be amazed at the sense of freedom and empowerment that comes with it. You will find yourself more energized, motivated, and focused on what truly matters in your life. You will be able to celebrate your wins, no matter how small, and learn from your mistakes, without getting bogged down in self-criticism or self-doubt.

I encourage you to look hard at the expectations you are holding onto in your life. Are they realistic and healthy, or are they holding you back from experiencing true freedom and growth? If the latter, let go of these expectations and set your sights on healthier, more achievable goals. The journey might be challenging, but the rewards will be well worth it.

Healthy Expectations Summary

1. Be realistic: Start by being realistic about what you can expect from yourself and others. Set achievable goals that align with your values and priorities, and avoid setting expectations that are too high or unrealistic.

2. Communicate clearly: Communicate your expectations clearly with others, whether it's in your personal or professional life. Be specific about what you hope to achieve and what you expect from others.

3. Be flexible: Healthy expectations require flexibility. Be willing to adjust your expectations if circumstances change, and be open to unexpected outcomes.

4. Focus on progress, not perfection: Instead of striving for perfection, focus on making progress towards your goals. Celebrate small successes along the way, and don't be too hard on yourself if things don't go exactly as planned.

5. Take responsibility: Take responsibility for your own actions and decisions, and avoid blaming others when things don't go as planned. This will help you to maintain a positive attitude and to stay focused on your goals.

6. Learn from setbacks: Setbacks and failures are a natural part of life. Instead of letting them discourage you, use them as an opportunity to learn and grow.

What Happens When You Lack Energy in Your Life

Listen up, warriors! If you lack energy in your life, it will impact every damn aspect of your existence. Your physical, mental, and emotional well-being will take a hit, and you won't be able to crush your everyday tasks, focus on your work or school, or engage in the activities that bring you joy.

Low energy makes you feel like a slug - tired, unmotivated, and apathetic. That's not a recipe for success, people. You must be fired up and ready to go if you want to make something of yourself.

But it's not just about feeling energized. If you're running on empty, you're also putting your health at risk. You'll struggle with sleep, weight management, and overall fitness and stamina, which can lead to some serious health issues down the line. And we don't want that, do we?

So, what's the solution? First, you must take care of yourself. Get enough sleep, eat a healthy diet, exercise regularly, manage your stress, limit the caffeine, and ditch the alcohol. Trust me; it's worth it.

But it's not just about physical self-care. We also must get our heads in the game. We must align our values with our actions, set clear goals, practice mindfulness, prioritize self-care, cultivate a positive mindset, manage our expectations, seek support, surround ourselves with positive people, and let go of those limiting beliefs.

By doing all this, we can boost our energy levels and live the life we deserve. So, let's do this, people! Let's get fired up and energized and make shit happen!

Self-Assessment Energetic Trait Questions

• On a typical day, how often do you feel energized and enthusiastic about your tasks and activities?

• How do you typically respond to challenging situations or obstacles that come your way? Do you tend to approach them with energy and determination, or do you feel defeated and drained?

• How do you prioritize your time and activities throughout the day? Do you tend to focus on high-energy tasks that require a lot of effort and engagement, or do you tend to avoid these types of activities?

• How do you motivate yourself to stay energized and engaged throughout the day? Do you have any specific techniques or strategies that you use to boost your energy levels?

• How do you feel about taking on new challenges or projects? Do you tend to approach these opportunities with energy and excitement, or do you feel overwhelmed and drained by the thought of trying something new?

• How do you handle stress and pressure in your daily life? Do you tend to let these factors drain your energy and motivation, or do you find ways to stay energized and focused even in difficult circumstances?

• How do you maintain your physical health and wellness? Do you prioritize regular exercise, a healthy diet, and adequate sleep to help keep your energy levels high?

• How do you approach your work and personal relationships? Do you tend to bring energy and enthusiasm to these interactions, or do you feel drained and disengaged?

• How do you feel about taking breaks and downtime throughout the day? Do you find that you need regular breaks to stay energized and focused, or do you tend to push through without taking time to recharge?

• How do you feel about your overall energy levels and enthusiasm for life? Do you feel energized and excited about your future, or do you feel drained and discouraged?

Your Energetic Action Steps

1. Exercise regularly: Regular exercise can increase your energy levels and improve your overall health. Find an activity that you enjoy and make it a part of your daily routine.

2. Get enough sleep: Make sure you are getting enough sleep each night. Most adults need 7-9 hours of sleep per night to feel rested and energized.

3. Drink plenty of water: Dehydration can cause fatigue and other health problems. Make sure you are drinking enough water throughout the day to stay hydrated.

4. Eat a healthy diet: Fuel your body with healthy, nutritious foods. Choose foods that are high in fiber, protein, and healthy fats to help sustain your energy levels throughout the day.

5. Take breaks: Take regular breaks throughout the day to recharge your energy levels. Go for a short walk, stretch, or take a few deep breaths to refresh your mind and body.

6. Manage stress: Stress can drain your energy levels. Find healthy ways to manage stress, such as meditation, yoga, or deep breathing exercises.

7. Listen to music: Listening to music can boost your energy levels and improve your mood. Create a playlist of upbeat songs to listen to when you need a quick energy boost.

8. Stay organized: Clutter and disorganization can be draining. Keep your living and work spaces organized to reduce stress and increase your energy levels.

9. Connect with others: Socializing with friends, family, or colleagues can boost your energy levels and improve your overall well-being.

10. Practice gratitude: Focus on the positive things in your life and express gratitude for them. Gratitude can improve your mood and increase your energy levels.

TRAIT #4: D = DRIVEN

"Drive is the fuel that powers the engine of success."
-Frederick Martinez

What is Drive?

Drive refers to a strong inner motivation or ambition to achieve a particular goal or set of goals. The internal force propels a person to take action and persist in the face of obstacles, setbacks, and challenges.

Various factors, such as personal values, interests, passions, and aspirations, can fuel drive. However, it often involves a deep sense of purpose or a desire to make a meaningful impact. Individuals with a strong drive are typically highly self-motivated, focused, and committed to their goals.

The drive can also be characterized by a willingness to take risks and push oneself beyond one's comfort zone to achieve success. It often involves high discipline, persistence, and resilience in the face of adversity.

Overall, the drive is a powerful force that can help individuals to achieve their goals and to make a meaningful impact in their personal and professional lives. Self-reflection, goal-setting, and focused action can cultivate and strengthen it.

What Does it Mean to be Driven?

Let me tell you what it truly means to be driven. It's about having a deep sense of purpose and a burning desire to achieve your goals no matter what it takes. It's about pushing yourself to the limit and even further. Being driven means being relentless in pursuing your passions and having the courage to take risks and overcome obstacles. It's about setting your sights on the horizon and never looking back. So, if you want to be driven, start by identifying your purpose and vision for your life. From there, let your passion and determination fuel you as you work towards achieving your goals. Remember, being driven isn't just about working hard - it's about working smart and never losing sight of what truly matters.

My Personal Story About Being Driven

Listen up, my friends. I've got a story to share that will light a fire under your butt. Like many of you, I've faced some tough times. I had to deal with learning disabilities and teachers who thought I was a lost cause. But I didn't let that stop me from achieving my dreams.

I knew that education was the key to unlocking my potential, so I set my sights on becoming an electrical engineer. And even though I had to take remedial classes and spent six long years in college, I never gave up. I knew that if I worked hard enough and refused to let adversity defeat me, I could achieve anything I wanted.

And boy, did I prove myself right. Today, I'm a successful engineer making a difference in the world and saving lives. I'm an international best-selling author whose words have inspired countless people to chase their dreams. And I'm a successful athlete representing my country on the world stage.

But here's the thing: my journey was challenging. I faced obstacles and challenges every step of the way. There were times when I was told to give up, drop a class, and admit defeat. But I refused to let those setbacks define me. Instead, I dug deep and found the strength to keep going.

One example of this was when I received a "D" on my first exam in electromagnetics. My professor told me to drop the class, but I knew I couldn't let that happen. So, I taught myself the material, pouring over textbooks and working through example exercises until I finally understood the concepts. And you know what? I passed the class with a B.

This experience taught me that anything is possible when we tap into our inner strength and refuse to give up. With the right mindset and a relentless drive to succeed, we can overcome any obstacle and achieve greatness. And that's what I want for you, my friends. So please believe in yourselves and your dreams, never give up, and keep pushing forward no matter what.

So, let's harness the power of drive within ourselves and chase our dreams relentlessly. Let's be our best selves and never abandon our passions and aspirations. With the right mindset and a never-say-die attitude, we can achieve anything we set our minds to. So, let's do this, my friends. Let's go out there and show the world what we're made of!

Driving with Purpose:
Fueling Your Passion for the Road Ahead

Alright, listen up, folks! It's time to dig deep and find out what makes you tick. What fuels your fire? What ignites your passion? What's your vision for the future? These questions will unlock your true potential and drive you toward success.

You see, nothing can stand in your way when you have a clear sense of purpose and a burning desire to achieve your goals. You'll be willing to put in the hard work, the late nights, and the sacrifices needed to make your dreams a reality.

So, take some time to reflect on what truly matters to you. Discover your passions, define your vision, and identify your purpose in life. Once you deeply understand these things, you'll have the motivation and drive to achieve anything you set your mind to.

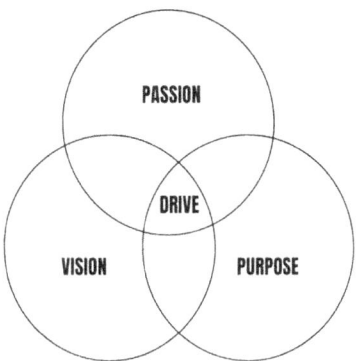

Passion is a crucial ingredient in the recipe for drive. When you're passionate about something, you're more likely to be motivated to work hard and see it through to the end.

Vision is also important. Having a clear picture of what you want to achieve can help you stay focused and motivated.

Purpose is the why behind which something is done. Having a sense of purpose or a higher goal that you're working towards can also help you stay driven. There's no one-size-fits-all answer for how to have drive and ambition. But if you can find your passion, vision, and purpose, you'll be well on your way to achieving great things.

Finding your passion, vision, and purpose is essential for being driven and achieving success. While it can be difficult to uncover what drives you, a few steps can help you get started.

Finding the Passion that Sets Your Heart on Fire

Hey there, my friend! Let's talk about the importance of finding your passion in life. It's the key to unlocking your full potential and living a fulfilling life. So, how do you discover your passion?

Ask yourself what activities bring you happiness, excitement, or fulfillment. You could do this for years, like playing an instrument or hitting the gym. Or, you may discover new passions by exploring different hobbies and skills.

But it's not just about discovering your passion; it's about prioritizing it in your life. Once you've identified something that brings you true happiness, prioritize it daily. This will keep you motivated and inspired and help you achieve your full potential.

Remember, my friend, there's no one-size-fits-all approach to finding your passion. It's a unique journey for everyone. But by staying curious, exploring new things, and following your heart, you'll be well on your way to discovering your true calling. So go out there, my friend, and live your best life!

Uncovering Your Vision for a Fulfilling Life

Oprah Winfrey once said, "Your vision is your mission in life. It's what you've put on this earth to do." And she's right. Your vision is what gives your life direction and purpose. So, how do you find your vision?

It starts by defining where you want to go in life. Think about the person you want to become and what you want to achieve. What are your dreams, aspirations, and values? Write them down and brainstorm ways to achieve them. Your vision doesn't have to be perfect; it can evolve as new opportunities arise.

But having a vision isn't enough. It would be best if you took action to make it a reality. To develop a plan of action and start taking steps towards your goal. Stay motivated by focusing on the result and challenging yourself along the way.

Remember, your vision is unique, so don't be afraid to dream big! And once you have your vision, the next step is to discover your purpose. What is the driving force that will propel you toward achieving your vision? Find that purpose and let it guide you toward a life of fulfillment and success.

So, my friend, define your vision, take action, and discover your purpose. With these tools, you can achieve anything you set your mind to.

Uncovering Your True Calling

Your purpose in life is the driving force that guides your actions and keeps you motivated towards achieving your goals. It is a deeply personal process that requires introspection and reflection. Here are some tips from successful individuals to help you find your purpose:

Start by identifying your talents, skills, and passions. What activities or pursuits bring you a sense of fulfillment and joy? What are you naturally good at, and what do you enjoy doing?

Reflect on your life experiences and the lessons you have learned from them. Consider the challenges you have overcome and how they have shaped you. These experiences can offer valuable insights into your purpose and passions.

Don't be afraid to seek advice and support from others who have found their purpose. Learn from their experiences and insights and apply them to your journey.

Remember that finding your purpose takes time and patience. It's a journey of self-discovery, and every step you take brings you closer to your true calling. So, stay focused on the big picture, and don't give up on yourself, even when times get tough.

Ultimately, your purpose in life is about making a difference in the world and positively impacting those around you. With a clear sense of purpose, you can stay motivated and inspired, even in the face of challenges and adversity. So, take the time to discover your purpose and start living a life of meaning and significance.

Drive Summary

1. Passion is a key ingredient for drive and motivation.

2. Vision provides direction and focus towards achieving your goals.

3. Purpose is the driving force behind what you do and helps you stay motivated towards your goals.

4. Finding your passion requires exploring activities that bring you happiness and fulfillment.

5. Uncovering your vision involves defining where you want to go in life, setting goals, and taking action towards achieving them.

6. Discovering your purpose involves identifying your talents, reflecting on your life experiences, seeking advice from others, and making a positive impact in the world.

What Happens When You Lack Drive in Your Life

Hey there, my friend! Let's talk about the power of drive and motivation in your life. With a burning desire and a sense of purpose, achieving your goals and reaching your full potential can be more accessible.

You may struggle to act and progress towards your dreams when you lack drive. It can leave you feeling lost and unsure of your direction. As a result, you may find yourself procrastinating and needing help to follow through on commitments and deadlines.

And let's remember the impact on your mental health and overall well-being. For example, a lack of drive can lead to feelings of apathy, boredom, and frustration, which can negatively affect your self-esteem and overall fulfillment in life.

But the good news is, my friend, there are strategies you can use to ignite your inner drive and motivation. One of the most powerful ways to do this is by setting clear goals and breaking down large tasks into smaller, more manageable ones. This will give you a sense of progress and momentum, fueling your motivation even further.

Seeking inspiration and guidance from others who have achieved similar goals can also be incredibly helpful. And remember to take care of yourself! Practicing self-care and maintaining a positive mindset can go a long way towards increasing your drive and motivation.

Remember, my friend, with the right mindset and strategies, you can overcome any obstacle and achieve your wildest dreams. So let's ignite that fire within you and unleash your full potential!

Self-Assessment Questions
On the Trait of Being Driven

• Am I self-motivated and proactive in pursuing my goals and aspirations?

• Do I have a clear vision of where I want to go and what I want to achieve in my life and career?

• Am I persistent and resilient in the face of setbacks and challenges?

• Do I have a plan for achieving my goals, and do I regularly take action towards them?

• Can I prioritize my time effectively, focusing on the most important tasks that will move me closer to my goals?

• Do I continuously seek out new knowledge and skills that will help me improve and achieve my goals?

• Do I hold myself accountable for my actions and take responsibility for my progress towards my goals?

• Can I stay focused and avoid distractions that may hinder my progress?

• Do I regularly evaluate my progress and adjust my approach to stay on track?

• Am I willing to take calculated risks and step out of my comfort zone to pursue my goals and aspirations?

Your Driven Action Steps

1. Set ambitious goals: Identify your long-term aspirations and set ambitious goals that align with them. Make sure your goals are specific, measurable, achievable, relevant, and time-bound.

2. Create a plan: Develop a detailed plan that outlines the steps you need to take to achieve your goals. Break down your plan into smaller, manageable steps to make it less overwhelming.

3. Stay focused: Stay focused on your goals and avoid distractions that may hinder your progress. Make sure you are working on the most important tasks first.

4. Take action: Take action every day towards your goals. Even small steps can add up over time and help you make progress towards your objectives.

5. Hold yourself accountable: Take responsibility for your actions and hold yourself accountable for your progress. Check in with yourself regularly to ensure you are on track.

6. Embrace challenges: Embrace challenges as opportunities to learn and grow. Use setbacks and failures as lessons to help you improve your approach and stay motivated.

7. Continuously learn: Continuously seek out new knowledge and skills that will help you improve and achieve your goals. Stay open-minded and curious.

8. Network: Connect with other driven individuals who share your interests and goals. Networking can help you gain new insights and opportunities.

9. Visualize success: Visualize yourself achieving your goals and how you will feel when you do. This can help you stay motivated and focused on your objectives.

10. Celebrate successes: Celebrate your successes, no matter how small. This can help you stay motivated and energized as you work towards your larger goals.

UNSTOPPABLE MINDSET

What is an Unstoppable Mindset?

Are you ready to take your life to the next level? An unstoppable mindset is the key to unlocking your full potential and achieving your goals. It's a state of mind that's defined by persistence, resilience, and a relentless attitude toward success. It's about constant growth, learning, and improvement, fueled by a profound purpose and passion.

But let's be honest - developing an unstoppable mindset isn't for the weak-willed. It takes grit, determination, and a willingness to push through obstacles and setbacks. It's about putting in the hard work, day in and day out, and never giving up on your dreams.

Luckily, there are some absolute powerhouses out there who can show you the way. From Mark Divine to Tony Robbins, Jocko Willink to Tim Grover, and Inky Johnson, these experts have mastered the art of focus, resilience, energy, and drive. In addition, they know that cultivating an unstoppable mindset requires discipline, consistency, and a commitment to excellence.

So, if you want to be the best version of yourself, then start following these legends. Immerse yourself in their teachings, absorb their motivation, and incorporate their strategies into your daily routine. With their guidance, you'll be well on your way to developing an unstoppable mindset that will propel you toward greatness.

What the Experts Say About Mindset

Mark Divine, Tony Robbins, Jocko Willink, Tim Grover, Inky Johnson are a few experts I follow to learn more about having an unstoppable mindset. Their teachings are infused with inspiration, motivation, and discipline:

Mark Divine is a retired Navy SEAL commander and founder of SEALFIT, a program designed to help individuals develop the mental and physical toughness of a Navy SEAL. Here's an example of an unstoppable mindset from Mark Divine's perspective:

"During my time in BUD/S (Basic Underwater Demolition/SEAL) training, I had a fellow SEAL trainee named Rick who was incredibly strong and fit. However, he lacked mental toughness and would often give up when faced with obstacles. One day, we were running a long-distance obstacle course called the O-Course, and Rick was struggling. He was ready to quit, but I knew that he had the physical ability to finish the course. I decided to run alongside him and push him to keep going. I reminded him of why he wanted to become a SEAL and what was at stake if he didn't finish the course. By the end of the O-Course, Rick was exhausted but had completed it. It was a defining moment for him and helped him develop the mental toughness needed to become a Navy SEAL."

Tony Robbins is a well-known motivational speaker and author. He has helped millions of people achieve success in various areas of their lives, including business, health, and relationships. Here's an example of an unstoppable mindset from Tony Robbins' perspective:

"I once had a client who was struggling to grow her business. She had a lot of setbacks and was about to give up when we had our first coaching session. I asked her to tell me about her biggest failure, and she shared a story about a time when she had lost everything. Her business had failed, she had lost her home, and her marriage had fallen apart. But instead of giving up, she used that failure as motivation to start again. She knew that she had hit rock bottom and that the only way to go was up. I encouraged her to use that same mindset to grow her current business. She went on to build a successful company and is now a millionaire. Her unstoppable mindset allowed her to turn her biggest failure into her greatest success."

Jocko Willink is a retired Navy SEAL commander and author of several books on leadership and discipline. Here's an example of an unstoppable mindset from Jocko Willink's perspective:

"During one of my deployments to Iraq, my SEAL team was tasked with taking a heavily fortified enemy position. We were vastly outnumbered, and the odds were not in our favor. But we knew that failure was not an option. We had trained for this moment, and we were prepared to do whatever it took to accomplish our mission. The battle was intense and lasted for hours, but we never wavered. We kept pushing forward, taking out enemy positions one by one. In the end, we emerged victorious. That experience taught me the power of an unstoppable mindset. When you believe in your mission and have the discipline to see it through, anything is possible."

Tim Grover is a renowned sports performance coach who has worked with some of the world's top athletes, including Michael Jordan, Kobe Bryant, and Dwyane Wade. Here's an example of an unstoppable mindset from Tim Grover's perspective:

"When I was working with Michael Jordan, he was known for his incredible work ethic and his unwavering commitment to winning. But what most people don't know is that he had an unstoppable mindset that drove him to be the best. He didn't just want to win; he wanted to dominate the competition. One time, during a game, he was struggling with his shooting. He missed several shots in a row, and most players would have let that get to them. But not Michael. He used that failure as motivation to work even harder. He kept shooting, even though he was missing, and eventually, he found his rhythm. By the end of the game, he had scored over 50 points and led his team to victory. That's the kind of mindset that separates the greats from the rest."

Inky Johnson is a motivational speaker and former college football player who frequently speaks about the power of mindset. He believes that our mindset determines our actions, and our actions ultimately shape our lives. Here is example of an unstoppable mindset of Inky Johnson telling his story:

"Growing up in a tough neighborhood in Atlanta, I knew from an early age that life was not going to be easy. But I refused to let my circumstances define me or hold me back. I was always determined to be the best I could be, no matter what challenges came my way. And when I discovered my passion for football, I knew that it was my ticket to a better life. I worked tirelessly, day in and day out, to perfect my craft. I trained harder than anyone else, and I refused to let failure or setbacks discourage me. I believed in myself and my abilities, and I knew that with hard work and determination,

I could achieve anything. And then, one day, everything changed. During a college football game, I suffered a devastating injury that left me paralyzed on one side of my body. In an instant, my dreams were shattered, and my future was uncertain. But even in that moment of darkness, I refused to give up. I refused to let my injury define me or limit my potential. Instead, I used it as a catalyst to inspire and motivate others. I became a motivational speaker, sharing my story with others and encouraging them to embrace their own potential and to never give up on their dreams. I saw my injury as an opportunity to make a difference in the world, and I refused to let it hold me back. Throughout my recovery and rehabilitation, I maintained a positive attitude and a strong work ethic. I refused to let my injury become an excuse for failure, and instead used it as a driving force to achieve my goals. For me, having an unstoppable mindset is about refusing to give up, no matter what obstacles come your way. It's about believing in yourself and your abilities, and having the courage to push through even the toughest challenges. It's about maintaining a positive attitude and a strong work ethic, and never losing sight of your dreams. Through my own example, I hope to inspire others to develop an unstoppable mindset and to never give up on their dreams, no matter what obstacles may come their way."

The stories from Inky Johnson, Tim Grover, Jocko Willink, Mark Divine, and Tony Robbins demonstrates an unstoppable mindset, then, is all about overcoming challenges, never giving up, and keeping a laser-like focus on your objectives. The discipline, mental toughness, and determination required to overcome obstacles and succeed may be found in people with this mindset, whether they work in the military, business, or sports.

Developing an Unstoppable Mindset

Alright, my friends, this is where the rubber meets the road. It's time to take all the wisdom we've gained from the previous chapters and put it into action. First, we've talked about the four crucial traits of an unstoppable mindset - focus, resilience, energy, and drive - and now it's time to combine them into a force that cannot be stopped.

Let's start with focus. We've learned that to develop a laser-like focus, we must break down our long-term objectives into manageable tasks and eliminate distractions. We need to use tools like time-blocking to structure our days and ensure we're dedicating enough time to each task.

Next up, resilience. We've learned that setbacks are inevitable, but we must bounce back, learn from our failures, and adapt to changing circumstances. We need to take care of ourselves, seek support from others, and keep pushing forward no matter what.

Energy is another critical component of an unstoppable mindset. We've learned to prioritize healthy habits like exercise, a balanced diet, sufficient sleep, and stress management. We need to recharge our emotional batteries by engaging in activities that bring us joy and fulfillment.

Last but not least, we've got drive. We've learned to identify our core values and use them to guide our decision-making and goal-setting. We need to set ambitious but achievable goals, break them down into actionable steps, and pursue them relentlessly, no matter what obstacles we face.

Combining all four traits - focus, resilience, energy, and drive - we can create an unstoppable force that propels us towards our goals with unrelenting intensity. But let's be clear - this is not a quick fix or an easy road. It takes consistent practice and a holistic approach to our physical, mental, and emotional well-being. But if we can master these four traits and cultivate an unstoppable mindset, nothing can stand in our way. So, let's get after it, my friends, and unleash our full potential!

Unstoppable Mindset Summary

1. The four crucial traits of an unstoppable mindset are focus, resilience, energy, and drive.

2. To develop laser-like focus, we need to break down long-term objectives into manageable tasks and eliminate distractions.

3. Setbacks are inevitable, but we need to bounce back, learn from our failures, and adapt to changing circumstances to build resilience.

4. Prioritizing healthy habits like exercise, balanced diet, sleep, and stress management is critical to maintaining high levels of energy.

5. Identifying core values and using them as a guiding force for decision-making and goal-setting is important to cultivate drive.

6. Combining these four traits creates an unstoppable force that propels towards goals with unrelenting intensity.

7. Mastering these traits takes consistent practice and a holistic approach to physical, mental, and emotional well-being.

8. Unleashing our full potential requires getting after it and cultivating an unstoppable mindset.

What Happens When You Don't Develop an Unstoppable Mindset

Let me tell you something, my friend. I'm about to drop some truth on you. If you want to unlock your true potential and achieve unparalleled success in life, then cultivating an unstoppable mindset is an absolute must. Without this mindset, you'll be like a ship without a rudder, adrift and directionless in the face of challenges.

You see, without an unstoppable mindset, you'll be prone to giving up too easily, succumbing to negative self-talk, and lacking the motivation to pursue your goals. And let me tell you, that's a surefire recipe for mediocrity.

If you don't develop an unstoppable mindset, you'll find yourself stuck in a cycle of self-doubt and self-sabotage, never realizing your true potential. And is that really what you want for yourself?

But if you're committed to greatness, then it's time to take control of your mindset and cultivate a resilient, determined, and optimistic attitude towards challenges and obstacles. With an unstoppable mindset, you'll be able to crush setbacks, smash through barriers, and achieve your wildest dreams.

Please don't settle for a mediocre life, my friend. Invest in yourself, commit to developing an unstoppable mindset, and watch as you rise to new levels of success and fulfillment. Remember, the only thing holding you back is your mindset.

Self-Assessment Questions
To Develop an Unstoppable Mindset

• Do you believe that obstacles and challenges are opportunities for growth and learning, rather than roadblocks to success?

• How do you respond to setbacks and failures? Do you give up easily or persist until you achieve your goal?

• Are you willing to take risks and step outside your comfort zone to pursue your goals?

• Do you have a clear and compelling vision for your life and future?

• Can you stay focused and motivated, even when faced with distractions or competing priorities?

• Do you actively seek new knowledge and skills to improve and achieve your goals?

• How do you handle criticism and feedback? Are you open to constructive criticism and willing to change based on feedback?

• Can you maintain a positive attitude and outlook, even in challenging situations?

• Do you surround yourself with people who support and encourage you, or do you allow negative influences to bring you down?

• How do you define success? Are you focused on achieving external rewards or motivated by a deeper sense of purpose and fulfillment?

Developing Unstoppable Mindset Action Steps

1. Set clear and achievable goals: Identify your goals and break them down into achievable steps. Make sure your goals are realistic but challenging.

2. Embrace failure: Instead of fearing failure, see it as an opportunity to learn and grow. Celebrate your mistakes and use them as opportunities to improve.

3. Take calculated risks: Be willing to step outside your comfort zone and take calculated risks. This will help you grow and develop new skills.

4. Practice persistence: When faced with setbacks or challenges, persist and keep working towards your goals. Don't give up easily.

5. Practice positive self-talk: Challenge negative self-talk and limiting beliefs with positive affirmations and thoughts. Believe in yourself and your abilities.

6. Continuously learn and improve: Seek out new knowledge and opportunities to learn and develop your skills. Be open to feedback and be willing to make changes based on it.

7. Stay focused and organized: Create a routine that helps you stay focused and organized. Prioritize your time and energy on your most important tasks and goals.

8. Surround yourself with positive people: Surround yourself with people who are positive, supportive, and encourage you to be your best self.

9. Practice self-care: Take care of your physical and mental health. Prioritize rest, exercise, and healthy habits to stay energized and focused.

10. Celebrate your successes: Don't forget to celebrate your successes, no matter how small. This will help you stay motivated and positive.

Strategies for Maintaining an Unstoppable Mindset

One must cultivate an unstoppable mindset unyielding to setbacks and challenges to achieve greatness in life. As discussed in the previous chapters, this requires a relentless commitment to personal growth, mental toughness, and unshakable resilience. However, it doesn't stop there once you develop an unstoppable mindset.

With that said, there are several steps that anyone can take to ensure that they maintain an unstoppable mindset. These four simple yet powerful strategies can help you cultivate a mindset that can weather any storm and overcome any obstacle life throws your way. By implementing these strategies, you can maintain an unstoppable mindset to help you achieve greatness and success in all areas of your life.

To maintain an unstoppable mindset, it's essential to cultivate an attitude of gratitude. Practicing gratitude means taking the time to recognize and appreciate the simple things in life that bring joy, such as the love and support of friends and family. Focusing on the positives in your life can help put the struggles and challenges you face into perspective, giving you the motivation and drive to keep pushing forward.

Gratitude is a powerful tool for fostering a positive and driven mindset. By recognizing the good things in your life, you can shift your focus away from negative thoughts and emotions, which can hold you back and make it difficult to move forward. Instead, you can channel your energy towards achieving your goals, taking on challenges, and pushing yourself to be the best version of yourself.

Developing gratitude practice doesn't mean ignoring or denying the challenges you face. Rather, it means proactively cultivating a positive and constructive mindset to help you tackle those challenges head-on. When you're grateful for the good things in your life, you can approach problems with a clear head and a more focused mindset, which can help you develop creative solutions and overcome obstacles.

Incorporating gratitude into your daily routine can be a simple yet powerful way to maintain an unstoppable mindset. You can start by setting aside time each day to reflect on the things in your life that you're grateful for, whether it's a supportive friend, a beautiful sunset, or a warm cup of coffee in the morning. Over time, this practice can help you develop a more positive and resilient mindset that's better equipped to handle whatever challenges life throws your way.

Ultimately, gratitude is a key component of maintaining an unstoppable mindset. By focusing on the good things in your life, you can foster a positive and driven mindset that's better equipped to handle challenges, overcome obstacles, and achieve your goals. So take some time today to reflect on the things you're grateful for in your life, and see how it can help you maintain an unstoppable mindset.

Maintaining strong connections with the people we love is crucial for developing an unstoppable mindset. A supportive network of family and friends can provide us with the motivation and encouragement to keep pushing forward during challenging times. As Tim Grover says, "success is not a solo sport," and having a strong support system can make all the difference in achieving our goals.

Moreover, sharing our emotions with others can help us cope with stress and handle difficult situations more constructively. By opening up to our loved ones about our fears, doubts, and challenges, we can gain valuable insights and perspectives to help us overcome obstacles and maintain a positive mindset. As David Goggins puts it, "vulnerability is the key to true strength."

In addition to providing emotional support, our loved ones can hold us accountable and keep us focused on our goals. By surrounding ourselves with people who share our values and ambitions, we can create a culture of excellence and push each other to be our best selves. As Ed Mylett says, "you are the average of the five people you spend the most time with," so surround yourself with people who inspire you and push you to improve.

Furthermore, staying connected with our loved ones can help us maintain balance and perspective. When we're consumed by work or other responsibilities, it's easy to lose sight of what's truly important. By staying connected with the people we care about, we can keep our priorities in check and ensure we live a fulfilling and meaningful life.

In short, building and maintaining strong relationships with our loved ones is a critical component of developing an unstoppable mindset. By surrounding ourselves with supportive, inspiring people, we can stay motivated and focused on our goals, handle challenges with greater resilience, and maintain a sense of balance and perspective.

Making regular exercise a habit is a non-negotiable step towards maintaining an unstoppable mindset. It's not just about looking good; it's about feeling good and performing at your best. Research has shown that exercise has numerous advantages beyond physical fitness. It can alleviate mental stress, improve concentration, boost resilience, and increase energy levels significantly.

As the saying goes, a healthy body equals a healthy mind. Exercise helps you look and feel better and has powerful mental health benefits. For example, regular exercise can help you manage stress and anxiety by releasing endorphins, the body's natural mood-boosting chemicals. This can improve your well-being and create a more positive and focused mindset.

Furthermore, exercise can also enhance your cognitive function, improving concentration and memory retention. It can help you stay sharp and alert, enabling you to tackle challenges more easily and efficiently. And by increasing your resilience and energy levels, exercise can help you power through difficult times with a never-say-die attitude.

In short, making exercise a habit is crucial for maintaining an unstoppable mindset. It can improve both your physical and mental health, making you better equipped to face any obstacle that comes your way. So, prioritize exercise in your daily routine, whether it's hitting the gym, running, or taking a yoga class. It's a small investment that can yield significant returns in your personal and professional life.

In the words of the greats like David Goggins and Tim Grover, "there are no shortcuts to success." Making regular exercise a habit is one of those non-negotiables that separates the winners from the losers. It's a crucial step towards achieving your goals and becoming the best version of yourself. So, get up, move, and start building an unstoppable mindset today.

Seeking inspiration from successful people is a powerful tool for cultivating an unstoppable mindset. Learning from those who have overcome seemingly insurmountable obstacles can be incredibly motivating and provide valuable insights on tackling challenges in your own life. Whether seeking advice from leaders in your field, reading biographies of successful individuals, or attending motivational events, surrounding yourself with stories of triumph can help keep you energized and focused on your goals.

As Tony Robbins has famously said, "success leaves clues." By studying successful individuals' habits, strategies, and mindsets, you can gain invaluable knowledge and insights into what it takes to achieve greatness. You can learn from their failures and successes, their setbacks and triumphs, and apply those lessons to your journey.

Moreover, seeking inspiration from successful people can help you stay motivated and committed to your personal and professional aspirations. When you're feeling discouraged or overwhelmed, hearing stories of others who have overcome similar challenges can help put things into perspective and remind you that hard work and persistence can make success possible.

In the words of Tim Grover, "don't just study success, create it." By seeking inspiration from successful individuals, you can gain the knowledge and tools you need to create your success story. As a result, you can develop the mental toughness and resilience necessary to overcome obstacles and achieve your goals.

So, whether it's reading books, attending seminars, or seeking out mentors, prioritize seeking inspiration from successful people in your pursuit of an unstoppable mindset. Let their stories fuel your drive and keep you focused on the path to success.

Strategies for Maintaining Unstoppable Mindset Summary

1. To achieve greatness in life, one must cultivate an unstoppable mindset that is unyielding to setbacks and challenges.

2. There are several steps that anyone can take to ensure that they maintain an unstoppable mindset.

3. Four simple yet powerful strategies can help you cultivate a mindset that can weather any storm and overcome any obstacle life throws your way.

4. To maintain an unstoppable mindset, it's essential to cultivate an attitude of gratitude.

5. Maintaining strong connections with the people we love is crucial for developing an unstoppable mindset.

6. Making regular exercise a habit is a non-negotiable step towards maintaining an unstoppable mindset.

7. Finally, maintaining an unstoppable mindset requires consistent effort and commitment. It's not something that happens overnight but rather a journey that requires ongoing personal growth, mental toughness, and unshakable resilience.

What Happens When You
Don't Maintain an Unstoppable Mindset?

My friend, let me tell you that maintaining an unstoppable mindset is crucial if you want to continue achieving success and reaching your full potential. However, more is needed to develop this mindset - you must also work to maintain it daily.

You see, life is full of ups and downs, and if you don't actively work to maintain your mindset, you'll be vulnerable to setbacks and failures. Furthermore, without an unstoppable mindset, you'll be more likely to give up, engage in negative self-talk, and lose motivation.

And let me tell you, my friend, that's a dangerous place to be. When you don't maintain an unstoppable mindset, you risk falling into a pattern of mediocrity and complacency. As a result, you'll miss out on opportunities, stop growing, and fail to reach your full potential.

But don't despair, my friend, because there are steps you can take to maintain your mindset. For example, you can surround yourself with positive influences, engage in daily affirmations and gratitude exercises, and consistently challenge yourself to grow and improve.

Remember, maintaining an unstoppable mindset is a daily practice. It requires discipline, focus, and commitment. But if you're willing to work, you'll reap the rewards of a life filled with success, fulfillment, and joy. So don't let yourself slip into a negative mindset - maintain your unstoppable attitude and keep pushing towards your dreams.

Self-Assessment Questions
To Maintain an Unstoppable Mindset

• How often do you reflect on your progress and achievements towards your goals? Do you celebrate your successes, no matter how small?

• How do you manage stress and setbacks? Are you able to stay focused and positive, even during challenging times?

• How do you prioritize your time and energy? Can you stay focused on your most important tasks and goals?

• How do you handle negative self-talk and limiting beliefs? Do you challenge them and replace them with positive affirmations and beliefs?

• How do you stay motivated and energized? Are you able to maintain a sense of purpose and passion for your goals?

• How do you stay adaptable and open to change? Are you willing to pivot and adjust your plans when necessary?

• How do you handle fear and uncertainty? Do you face them head-on or avoid them?

• How do you stay connected to your support system? Do you regularly seek out feedback, advice, and encouragement from others?

• How do you practice self-care and maintain your physical and mental health? Do you prioritize rest, exercise, and healthy habits?

• How do you stay committed to your personal and professional growth? Do you continually seek out new challenges and opportunities to learn and develop your skills?

Maintaining Unstoppable Mindset Action Steps

1. Reflect on your progress and achievements: Take time to reflect on your progress and achievements towards your goals. Celebrate your successes, no matter how small.

2. Practice positive self-talk: Challenge negative self-talk and limiting beliefs with positive affirmations and thoughts. Believe in yourself and your abilities.

3. Prioritize self-care: Take care of your physical and mental health. Prioritize rest, exercise, and healthy habits to stay energized and focused.

4. Stay connected with your support system: Stay connected with your support system, seek out feedback, advice, and encouragement from others.

5. Stay focused on your goals: Keep your goals in mind and prioritize your time and energy on your most important tasks.

6. Practice persistence: When faced with setbacks or challenges, persist and keep working towards your goals. Don't give up easily.

7. Practice adaptability: Stay adaptable and open to change. Be willing to pivot and adjust your plans when necessary.

8. Stay motivated and energized: Stay motivated and energized by finding ways to stay connected to your purpose and passion.

9. Seek out new challenges and opportunities: Continuously seek out new challenges and opportunities to learn and develop your skills.

10. Celebrate your successes: Don't forget to celebrate your successes, no matter how small. This will help you stay motivated and positive.

How Michael Jordan Developed Unstoppable Mindset

Michael Jordan is widely regarded as one of the greatest basketball players ever. His success on the court is a testament to his mastery of the four essential traits for an unstoppable mindset: focus, resilience, energy, and drive. Here's a real-life example of how Jordan embodied these qualities to achieve greatness:

Throughout his career, Jordan was known for his intense focus on basketball. He often spent hours studying his opponents' tendencies and practicing his moves, constantly striving to improve his skills. This focus helped him become one of the most dominant players in the sport's history and allowed him to consistently perform at an elite level.

In addition to his focus, Jordan was also incredibly resilient. He faced many setbacks throughout his career, including injuries, personal tragedies, and intense scrutiny from the media and fans. However, he always bounced back from these challenges with renewed determination and a stronger sense of purpose. For example, after being cut from his high school basketball team, Jordan worked tirelessly to improve his skills and eventually became a star player at the University of North Carolina.

Jordan's energy and drive were also essential to his success. He was known for his relentless work ethic, often practicing for hours and pushing himself to the limit in every game. He was always striving to be the best, and his dedication to his craft enabled him to succeed.

Michael Jordan's mastery of focus, resilience, energy, and drive helped him become an unstoppable force on the basketball court. His unwavering commitment to excellence and his ability to overcome adversity inspire anyone seeking to achieve their goals and reach their full potential.

Conclusion

Developing an unstoppable mindset is a continuous journey and a lifestyle that necessitates a focused, resilient, energetic, and driven approach. It is essential to focus your energy and attention on setting specific goals and taking meaningful action steps daily. It is also vital to remain resilient in the face of obstacles and setbacks; do not become discouraged by missed opportunities or mistakes, but instead embrace them as learning experiences and use them to refine and strengthen your goals. Finally, you must maintain a purposeful attitude and transfer that energy into making daily positive progress.

It requires a combination of focus, resiliency, energy, and drive to achieve success. Focus helps us to stay on track and maintain momentum towards our goals. Resilience enables us to bounce back from difficult situations and remain focused on our objectives despite adversity. Energy keeps us motivated and driven towards self-improvement, pushing us to go further than ever before. Finally, drive means setting ambitious goals for ourselves and pursuing them with passion and determination until they are achieved.

An unstoppable mindset is a lifelong pursuit that demands unwavering focus, resilience, energy, and drive. Concentrating your focus and efforts towards defining clear goals and taking consistent action towards their attainment is crucial. Resilience plays a key role in overcoming challenges and setbacks, transforming them into valuable learning experiences that only enhance your goals. The drive to self-improvement must be powered by a high energy level, which keeps you motivated and pushing forward toward your aspirations. A purposeful attitude must be maintained to make steady progress toward your objectives and achieve success through focus, resilience, energy, and drive.

Mastering oneself is a challenging task, but it is worth the effort. You can achieve the unstoppable mindset you desire by taking small steps each day toward achieving your goals and using these four key elements as your guide. Remember that an unstoppable mindset is a journey and not a destination, so enjoy every step of the process. With consistency and dedication, you can achieve the unstoppable mindset you desire.

Celebrating your successes along the way and rewarding yourself for your hard work is also important. Don't fear setbacks or failures; use them as learning opportunities to grow even stronger in pursuing your goals. Believe in yourself and take action towards reaching success. With a consistent focus, resilience, energy, and drive, you can achieve an unstoppable mindset and become the best version of yourself.

Appendix: Additional Information to Help Achieve an Unstoppable Mindset

Finding Your Flow State

The flow state, or "being in the zone," is the mental state where an individual is fully engaged and focused on a task, and everything else fades away. In this state, individuals can perform at their highest level and achieve their best results.

Tim Grover is a renowned performance coach who has worked with some of the world's greatest athletes, including Michael Jordan, Kobe Bryant, and Dwyane Wade. His philosophy on the flow state, also known as being in the zone, involves several fundamental principles.

Grover believes that there are several fundamental principles to achieving the flow state, including:

Focus: The athlete must focus entirely on their performance and block out any distractions or external factors that could impact their performance.

Preparation: The athlete must have prepared thoroughly for their performance and be confident in their abilities.

Mindset: The athlete must have a positive, confident mindset and believe they can achieve their goals.

Trust: The athlete must trust their instincts and training and be willing to take risks to achieve their goals.

Intensity: The athlete must have a high level of intensity and be willing to push themselves to their limits to achieve their best performance.

By following these principles, Grover believes that athletes can achieve the flow state and perform at their highest level. However, he also acknowledges that achieving the flow state is not easy and requires much hard work, dedication, and practice.

Have there ever been times when you got so caught up in a task that you lost all sense of time? The environment around you vanished under the weight of your focused concentration, leaving only the task at hand.

How often do you experience what I just described? My guess would be very few. Yet, most of us find ourselves extremely distracted when we try to do our work.

That state is called the "flow state." If you want to achieve maximum productivity and maximum satisfaction in your day-to-day tasks, knowing how to get into this heightened state is important. It's the game changer that sets you apart from everyone else.

What is the Flow State?

The flow state is when you are completely absorbed in what you're doing, achieving immense satisfaction from your work. Everything else fades into the background, and your attention is entirely focused on that object.

To enter this state, you must be 100% engaged and fully committed to the task. Your mind and body are occupied, leaving no room for other distractions, worries, or tasks. You'll be so focused that nothing can distract you from the job in front of you.

The benefits of the Flow State are significant. You'll experience total immersion, increased productivity, no distractions, and lose track of time. You'll enjoy the task and stretch yourself by tackling worthy and challenging goals. As a result, you'll live a more meaningful life, dedicating your time to tasks that bring joy and meaning.

So, choose a task that requires your full attention, set clear goals, eliminate distractions, and immerse yourself in the task. Then, get ready to experience the bliss of Flow State!

How to Enter the Flow State

To truly enter the flow state, it's important to choose a challenging task that is both worthy and significant. You want to aim for a goal that will stretch you to the maximum and require you to use all your skills and abilities. Your purpose for entering the flow state is to positively impact the world, to achieve something noble and meaningful that will leave a lasting legacy.

Focus on the ONE thing that will make the biggest difference when you accomplish it. This should be a goal that requires your full attention and demands your full engagement. Don't settle for something easy or trivial; choose a task that will push you to your limits and allow you to unleash your true potential.

Setting clear goals for what you want to achieve. You need to be specific about what you want to accomplish during a certain period of time. By doing so, you force yourself to concentrate and avoid wasting time.

To make the most of your time, it's important to use boundaries and focus on one thing at a time during your period of intense concentration. I highly recommend using the Time Quarter Motion Method, where you concentrate for 25 minutes without distractions and then take a 5-minute break.

But here's a crucial point: you must give yourself enough time to get into the flow state. If you have to stop working in just a few minutes, it's not enough time to fully immerse yourself in your task. So, choose your goals and time frames wisely, and watch your productivity skyrocket!

Cut out all distractions. Put your phone on airplane mode, close your email, and silence all notifications. If necessary, block social media sites that might distract you. Listen to background music that will drown out any distracting conversations.

Your goal in all of this is to clear away anything that might distract your attention from the task. Remember, you aim to give 100% of your focus to a single task. If anything cuts into that focus, it needs to be eliminated. You must be extremely vigilant about this.

Distractions can disrupt your flow and prevent you from achieving peak performance. So, my friend, make it a habit to eliminate all distractions before you start working on a task. You'll find it easier to enter the flow state and achieve your goals with practice and consistency.

To enter the flow state, you must eliminate all multitasking. Trying to work on multiple things at once can be tempting, but doing so will kill your flow. To achieve the flow state, you must focus, drive, and energy on one thing.

You must become so fully immersed in one task that all other distractions fade away. This can't happen if you're simultaneously trying to work on a sales report, chat with coworkers on Skype, respond to emails, and text your spouse about dinner.

If you respect your work and want to do it with excellence, you must stop multitasking. Your brain simply doesn't have enough power to focus on multiple things at the same time. Instead, to enter the flow state, you must focus on one task.

So, my friend, eliminate multitasking from your life and focus on one task at a time. With practice and persistence, you'll find that you can enter the flow state more efficiently and achieve peak performance in your work.

Distractions can make giving 100% of yourself to the task at hand challenging.

So, how can you ensure that your concentration is at peak capacity? One of the primary ways is by getting enough sleep. High-performers know that sleep is essential for peak performance. So, they establish good sleep habits, go to bed at a reasonable hour, and wake up feeling refreshed and energized.

But what if you need an extra jolt of concentration during the day? Well, one option is to drink coffee or tea shortly before entering the flow state. Caffeine can aid your brain in concentrating and boost you to enter the flow state.

Remember, strengthening your concentration is key to entering the flow state. So, make sure to prioritize getting enough sleep and consider using caffeine as a tool to aid your concentration. With these tips, you'll be well on your way to achieving peak performance and creating unstoppable momentum.

Are you struggling to enter the flow state? It could be that your emotions are getting in the way. Emotions like anger, frustration, worry, or overwhelm can make concentrating and entering the flow state hard.

If you are in this situation, step back and monitor your emotional state. It's essential to be aware of your emotions because they can significantly impact your ability to enter the flow state. For example, if you're feeling extremely angry or overwhelmed, it might be necessary to do some work to calm down first.

Remember, your emotional state can govern whether or not you can enter the flow state. So, take the time to check in with yourself regularly and make sure you're in the right emotional state before you try to enter the flow state. By doing so, you'll be setting yourself up for success and maximizing your potential for peak performance.

Are you ready to learn more about the power of anchoring and creating a flow state ritual? Let me tell you, this can be a game-changer for your performance and productivity!

When you're seeking to enter the flow state, one thing that can be extremely helpful in creating a ritual or series of actions you perform every single time. This can be anything that works for you, such as taking a few deep breaths, listening to a specific song, or doing a quick stretch.

Here's the key: I cannot emphasize enough how crucial it is to consistently repeat your flow state ritual. Every time you perform this ritual, your body and brain associate these actions with entering a state of optimal performance. This is the magic of anchoring at work.

The more you repeat this ritual, the more powerful the association becomes, and the easier it is to enter the flow state. It's like training a muscle - the more you exercise it, the stronger it gets.

By consistently performing your flow state ritual, you're training your body and brain to enter this state of peak performance more easily and effortlessly. And the best part is that you can do this anytime, anywhere, and in any situation.

My friend, creating a flow state ritual can be a game-changer for your performance and productivity. So, experiment with your ritual today; find something that works for you, and repeat it whenever you want to enter the flow state. Keep up the excellent work, and stay consistent with your flow state ritual. By doing so, you're training your body and brain to perform at their best, and you'll be amazed at the results you can achieve. With practice, you'll find it easier and easier to enter this state of peak performance, and you'll be able to unleash your true potential. So, let's continue to take action toward our goals and create unstoppable momentum together!

Use the Time Quarter Motion Method to Focus on the Task

The Time Quarter Motion Method is similar to the Pomodoro technique but differs in that the breaks involve physical activity to get the blood pumping in your body. This method uses a timer to divide work into 25-minute intervals, known as "quarters," followed by short breaks. After four quarters, a longer break of 15-30 minutes is taken. The key idea behind this method is that frequent breaks with movement can improve mental agility and productivity.

Compared to the Pomodoro technique, the Time Quarter Motion Method offers several benefits:

1. Being active during breaks can increase blood flow and oxygenation, which enhances alertness and mental clarity.

2. Physical activity can reduce stress and anxiety levels, which can be a significant distraction when trying to focus.

3. Exercise can release endorphins, promoting relaxation and concentration.

4. The movement has been linked to improved mood and increased overall well-being.

5. Taking a break with movement can provide a change of scenery, breaking the monotony of sitting at a desk and offering a refreshing change of pace.

Overall, incorporating movement into breaks can be a great way to maintain focus and increase productivity, and the Time Quarter Motion Method offers a unique approach to achieving these benefits. Whether going for a walk, doing some yoga, or even just stretching, taking a break with movement can help you stay focused and productive throughout the day.

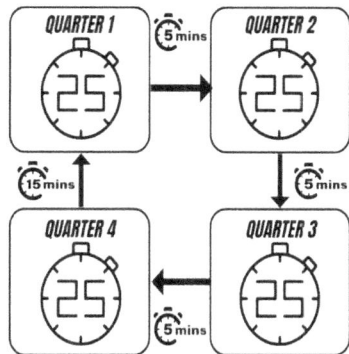

Here's How the Time Quarter Motion Method Works:

• Set a timer for 25 minutes and work intensely (no distractions) for those 25 minutes.

•After 25 minutes, take a minute 5 exercise break to let your brain rest. During those five minutes, you can do whatever exercise you want.

•Then do another 25-minute session followed by another 5-minute exercise break.

•After four 25-minute sessions, take a 15-minute exercise and decompress break.

•Repeat the process.

Note: The Time Quarter Method requires you to concentrate intensely for 25 minutes without interruptions, enabling you to enter the focus flow state. It's crucial to allocate sufficient time to reach this state. During breaks, take a brief stroll around the neighborhood, perform push-ups and air squats, or engage in any movement activity and get away from your desk for a few minutes. Regular breaks can help you remain invigorated and attentive to the task.

The Power of Breathwork: Unleashing Your Unstoppable Potential

Breathwork is one of the most transformative tools for personal growth and development. It has the power to calm your mind, energize your body, and connect you with your innermost desires. When you master the art of breathing, you can become unstoppable in all areas of your life.

In this chapter, we'll explore the benefits of breathwork and different breathing techniques you can use to unleash your unstoppable potential.

Benefits of Breathwork

Breathwork is a powerful tool that can help you overcome stress, anxiety, and other mental and physical challenges. Here are just a few of the benefits you can experience through regular breathwork practice:

Increased Energy: Breathwork can increase energy levels and boost overall vitality. By breathing deeply and consciously, you can increase the flow of oxygen to your brain and body, which can help you feel more alert and focused.

Reduced Stress and Anxiety: One of the most significant benefits of breathwork is its ability to reduce stress and anxiety. When you breathe deeply and slowly, you activate your body's relaxation response, which can help calm your mind and body.

Improved Sleep: Breathwork can also enhance the quality of your sleep. Practicing slow, deep breathing before bed can help your body and mind relax, leading to more restful sleep.

Enhanced Physical Performance: Breathwork can improve physical performance by increasing lung capacity and endurance. By practicing breathing exercises, you can learn to breathe more efficiently, which can help you perform better in sports, training, and other physical activities.

Types of Breathing Techniques

There are many different types of breathing techniques you can use to unlock your unstoppable potential. Here are a few of the most effective ones:

Diaphragmatic Breathing: Diaphragmatic breathing, also known as belly breathing, is a simple and effective technique for reducing stress and anxiety. To practice this technique, breathe deeply through your nose, filling your belly with air as you inhale. Next, exhale slowly through your mouth, emptying your belly of air.

Box Breathing: Box breathing is a powerful technique that can help you calm your mind and increase your focus. To practice this technique, inhale through your nose for four counts, hold your breath for four counts, exhale through your mouth for four counts, and hold your breath for four counts. Repeat this cycle for several minutes.

Alternate Nostril Breathing: Alternate nostril breathing is a technique that can help you balance your energy and calm your mind. To practice this technique, sit comfortably and place your right thumb over your right nostril. Inhale deeply through your left nostril, then close your left nostril with your ring finger and exhale through your right nostril. Next, Inhale through your right nostril, then close it with your thumb and exhale through your left nostril. Repeat this cycle for several minutes.

Breath of Fire: Breath of Fire is a potent method that may energize your body and boost your vitality. To perform this technique, find a comfortable seat and quickly inhale and exhale through your nose while maintaining an equal length inhale and exhale without delay between breaths. If you master the breath of fire, you should be able to breathe in and out two to three times per second. Keep your motions rhythmic and regular, and concentrate on breathing from your diaphragm.

Holotropic Breathing: Begin breathing deeply and rapidly through your mouth without pausing between inhales and exhales. Depending on the session, this should be done for 20 to 30 minutes or longer. Once the breathwork is complete, allow yourself to relax and breathe naturally. The facilitator may play music or offer guidance to help you deepen your experience. After the session, take some time to reflect on your experience and integrate any insights or emotions that arose during the session. You should journal or talk to the facilitator or other participants about your experience.

It is important to note that holotropic breathing can be a powerful and intense experience and should only be done under the guidance of a trained facilitator. In addition, it may not be suitable for everyone, particularly those with certain medical conditions, so it is important to consult a healthcare professional before trying this technique.

Wim Hof Breathing: Start by taking 30 to 40 deep breaths in succession, inhaling deeply, and exhaling each time fully. Breaths should be taken in through the nose and out through the mouth without pausing between inhales and exhales. Hold your breath after the last exhale; hold your breath for as long as you comfortably can. The goal is to hold your breath for at least 1 minute, but you should only do what feels comfortable. When you can no longer hold your breath, exhale fully and take a deep breath in. Hold this breath for 10-15 seconds, then exhale and return to normal breathing. Repeat this cycle of deep breaths followed by breath holding for several rounds or until you feel a sense of relaxation and invigoration.

The Wim Hof Breathing Technique is said to have a range of benefits, including increased energy, reduced stress, improved focus and concentration, and increased immune system function. However, it is important to note that, as with any breathing technique, it may not be suitable for everyone and should be done under the guidance of a qualified practitioner.

Uses of Breathwork to Become Unstoppable

You can become unstoppable in all areas of your life with breathwork. These are some techniques for using breathwork to reach your full potential:

Increase Your Confidence: By relaxing your body and mind and making you feel more grounded and centered, breathwork can help you feel more confident.

Boost Your Creativity: Breathwork can also promote creativity by increasing the oxygen supply to your brain and enhancing your ability to access your creative potential. By practicing breathwork before engaging in creative pursuits, you can increase your capacity for innovative creativity.

Improve Your Focus: By calming your mind and assisting you in tuning out distractions, breathing exercises can also help you focus better. Before starting a task that demands concentration, try some breathwork to improve your capacity to stay focused and productive.

Manage Your Emotions: By enabling you to connect with your innermost feelings and release any tension or stress you might be hanging onto, breathwork can help you regulate your emotions. As a result, you can regain balance and clarity by engaging in breathwork when you're experiencing stress or overwhelmed.

Increase Your Resilience: Breathwork can also improve your resilience by developing an awareness of your inner calmness and strength. You can improve the capacity to easily overcome challenges and rebound from setbacks by consistently engaging in breathwork.

Breathwork is a tremendous tool that can help you realize your limitless potential. You may boost your energy, relieve tension and anxiety, and improve your physical and mental performance by engaging in various breathing exercises. Breathwork can assist you in achieving your objectives and becoming the best version of yourself, whether you want to develop your creativity, boost your self-confidence, or control your emotions. So, exhale deeply and prepare to unleash your limitless potential!

How to Have a Clear Sense of Personal and Self-Identity

I want to share a subject essential to shaping who we are as individuals - personal identity and self-identity. These two concepts are often used interchangeably, but they are quite distinct and greatly impact our ability to achieve our goals and reach our full potential.

So, what is the difference between personal identity and self-identity? Personal identity refers to the unique characteristics and traits that define us as individuals - our skills, talents, experiences, and values. Conversely, self-identity refers to the beliefs and values we hold about ourselves and our place in the world. In other words, personal identity is what we are, while self-identity is who we believe ourselves to be. Personal and self-identity can help you to clarify your values, interests, and goals, which can, in turn, make it easier to maintain focus and motivation. When you clearly understand what is important to you and what you want to achieve, it can be easier to prioritize your time and energy accordingly.

Understanding these distinctions is important because personal identity and self-identity work in tandem to create who we are as individuals. When we have a strong sense of personal identity, we can recognize and appreciate our unique qualities and strengths. This, in turn, helps us develop a positive self-identity based on our beliefs and values rather than external expectations or societal norms.

Personal identity traits, qualities, or attributes are features that characterize an individual and give them uniqueness. Typical aspects of one's personal identity include:

• Physical appearance: These include traits including height, weight, eye and hair colors, body shape, and facial features.

• Personality: This refers to a person's distinctive thought, feeling, and behavior tendencies. It encompasses qualities like extroversion, introversion, empathy, kindness, honesty and openness.

• Skills and abilities: This includes a person's abilities, skills, and knowledge. For instance, someone might be good at playing the piano, have a knack for writing, or know a lot about a certain topic.

• Values and beliefs: They make up a person's worldview and moral and ethical values. They may include religious beliefs, political beliefs, and philosophical views.

• Life experiences: These are the events and situations that influence a person's life. These could include things like travel, education, employment, interpersonal relationships, and personal difficulties.

• Social identity: This includes aspects of a person's identity that are shaped by their social group, such as race, ethnicity, gender, sexual orientation, and cultural background.

Each of these personal identity characteristics influences how a person interacts with their world around them and develops a sense of self. Self-identity traits are the features that constitute one's sense of identity. The characteristics, beliefs, attitudes, and experiences that make a person special and set them apart from others. Many typical self-identity traits include:

• Self-awareness: This relates to a person's capacity to comprehend their ideas, feelings, and actions as well as their influence on their behavior.

• Self-esteem: This has to do with a person's perception of their own value and how they see themselves in comparison to other people.

• Self-confidence: This speaks to a person's confidence in their skills and readiness to accept challenges.
• Personal values: These are the values and beliefs that a person holds to be important. They may include things such as honesty, respect, and compassion.

• Beliefs and attitudes: These are a person's views on various subjects, including religion, politics, and social issues.

• Goals and aspirations: These are the things that a person wants to achieve in their life, whether they are related to career, relationships, personal growth, or other areas.

• Past experiences: These are the events and situations that have shaped a person's life and have contributed to their sense of self.

All of these self-identity traits combine to form a person's sense of self, and they impact how that person sees themselves and interacts with others.

Let me share a personal experience that illustrates the power of personal and self-identity in developing an unstoppable mindset. I sustained a terrible injury a few years ago that left me unable to walk pain-free for months, my foot numb, and every step I took radiating pain from my glute to my feet. This was a devastating blow for me, personally, professionally, and athletically. However, since I've built my life living an ideal healthy lifestyle, I always look forward to challenging my limits in Olympic Lifting events. I had always led by example, encouraging people to accomplish their goals and overcome challenges, but suddenly, I was forced to rely on others and ask for their assistance.

I was initially devastated. I felt like I had lost a piece of myself, and I was unsure how to proceed. I asked my friends and trainers for suggestions. I utilized my resources and sought advice from every medical practitioner who treats elite athletes. I believed that if they could fix my back and take out the herniated discs, I would be able to resume my training in time to compete for the United States in the Master's World Weightlifting Championships, which would take place in a year and a half. Instead of telling me what I needed to hear, I wanted the physicians to tell me what I wanted to hear. They told me my Olympic lifting career was over unless I wanted to receive a spinal fusion in the future.

Many nights in bed were spent thinking about how much I would rather die than lose the last thing I loved. When I lost my mom to pulmonary fibrosis, my dad to pancreatic cancer, and my son to holoprosencephaly, my business failed, and I lost my marriage and business; this sport helped me cope. Olympic Lifting was the one sport in which I felt like I could do anything and was unstoppable. I was average at best when I competed in other sports, but when I got onto the platform for weightlifting, I felt like I went from being the underdog to a champion. I always felt in the zone because it was just me and the weights.

Following my little moment of self-pity, I put on my big boy pants. Collaborating with my physical therapists, we developed a strategy for preparing for the international competition. Unfortunately, I experienced a significant setback and started to experience numbness in both of my feet after having a "come to Jesus" moment. I stopped overhead lifting, underwent some rehabilitation, and was able to regain sensation in both of my feet.

When I went on a short trip to Cancun during the Thanksgiving holiday, I bounced around and danced, enjoying the moment and my newfound freedom from pain. The moment I understood, I didn't have to be defined by my injury. Instead, to create a new sense of self-identity centered on discovering new possibilities rather than obsessing over my limits, I focused on my identity—my abilities, knowledge, and experience.

I started exploring different approaches to leading a healthy lifestyle, maintaining my physical fitness, and competing, pushing myself beyond my comfort zone. I participated in a physique competition and placed first in my age group and second overall. Through red-light treatment, hot sauna therapy, cold immersion therapy, breathwork, meditation, and a more anti-inflammatory diet, I began to find strategies to lessen the inflammation in my back. I also asked for assistance and support from others, which was challenging for me initially but ultimately aided in developing stronger bonds and partnerships.

I found a new sense of resilience and purpose via this process that I had never known I had. I saw that my injury was not a constraint but a chance to change and advance. And that, my friends, is the power of the self and the self-identity in creating an unstoppable mindset.

Thus, please spend some time considering your own identity as a person. What differentiates you? What values and passions do you hold?

How can you use these traits to strengthen your sense of self and create an unstoppable mindset? Keep in mind that you can determine who you are and build the life you desire.

One of the most important lessons to be learned from my tale is how crucial it is to change our viewpoint when we encounter difficulties or setbacks. It might be too simple to adopt a victim mentality, feel sorry for ourselves, and concentrate on our shortcomings. But by concentrating on our individuality and the traits that make us distinctive, we may change our perspective and see difficulties as chances for development.

The capacity to let go of outdated self-identities restricting us is another crucial component in creating an unstoppable attitude. We have self-perceived values and beliefs, some of which may be constrictive or out-of-date. For instance, you might have always felt that you lacked "creativity" or were bad at public speaking.

But the truth is, these beliefs are often based on past experiences or external feedback rather than our inherent qualities or potential. By challenging these beliefs and opening ourselves up to new possibilities, we can create a new self-identity more aligned with our true potential.

One exercise that can be helpful in this process is to ask yourself: "Who would I be if I didn't believe [insert limiting belief here]?" For example, "Who would I be if I didn't believe I was not creative?" By imagining a new possibility, we can let go of old self-identities and create a more empowering and unstoppable mindset.

Finally, creating a strong sense of self-identity is essential to creating an unstoppable mindset. We may develop a new sense of purpose, resilience, and authenticity that will enable us to overcome any challenge and accomplish our goals by acknowledging and respecting our special characteristics and strengths, confronting limiting beliefs, and changing our old self-identities. Remember that you can define who you are and design the life you choose. To succeed and find fulfillment, set out and create an unstoppable mindset.

The Eisenhower Matrix

To achieve excellence in your work, it's important to prioritize your tasks and eliminate the need for multitasking. This is because multitasking can hinder productivity and prevent you from achieving your goals.

One effective tool for prioritizing tasks is the Eisenhower matrix. This matrix categorizes tasks based on their urgency and importance and consists of four quadrants.

The first quadrant is for urgent and important tasks that should be addressed immediately. The second quadrant is for tasks that are important but not urgent and should be scheduled later. The third quadrant is for urgent but unimportant tasks, which can often be delegated to someone else. Finally, the fourth quadrant is for tasks that are neither urgent nor important and can be eliminated or postponed.

Using the Eisenhower matrix to prioritize your tasks, you can focus your energy on the most important and urgent tasks first while scheduling less urgent tasks for later. This can help you to eliminate the need for multitasking, allowing you to give each task your full attention and achieve excellence in your work.

Why would you want to multitask when trying to get the most important work done with excellence?

The Eisenhower matrix is a tool that can be used to prioritize tasks by categorizing them according to their level of urgency and importance. The matrix consists of four quadrants, each representing a different priority level.

The quadrants are labeled as follows:

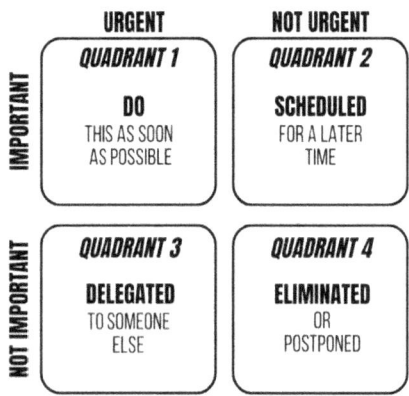

Using the Eisenhower matrix method, start by listing all your tasks on paper or in a digital task manager. Then, categorize each task according to the quadrant it belongs in. Once you have done this, focus on completing the tasks in quadrant one first, as these are the most important and require immediate attention. After you have completed the tasks in Quadrant 1, move on to the tasks in Quadrant 2.

It's also important to note that you should delegate tasks in Quadrant 3 as much as possible and avoid tasks in Quadrant 4. This way, you can focus on the most important task and work towards your goal with a clear mind.

Once you use the Eisenhower matrix method to categorize your tasks into quadrants based on their level of urgency and importance will help you focus on the most important tasks first and eliminate the tendency to multitask.

Set specific goals for each task and ensure they align with your priorities. This will help you to stay focused and motivated throughout the day.

Use a timer or a productivity app to track your progress and stay on task. This will help you stay accountable and ensure you are making the most of your time.

Evaluate your progress regularly and make adjustments as needed. This will help you to stay on track and achieve your goals in a timely manner.

Multitasking can be a major source of distraction and can make it difficult to get the most important work done with excellence. However, by using the Eisenhower matrix method to prioritize your tasks and set specific goals, you can stay focused and maximize your time. Additionally, setting a specific time for distractions, saying no to additional work, and evaluating progress regularly, can help eliminate multitasking and ensure you maximize your time and energy.

Communication Skills

Adopting good communication skills based on NLP (Neuro-Linguistic Programming), Dale Carnegie's principles, and the Navy SEALs ethos can involve several steps.

Firstly, it's essential to understand the other person's perspective. NLP teaches that effective communication is about understanding the other person's perspective and using language that resonates with them. This means actively listening to what they have to say and trying to understand their point of view.

Secondly, use positive language. Dale Carnegie's principle of "using a person's name" is a powerful tool for effective communication. Using someone's name in conversation makes them feel important and valued. Also, using positive language and avoiding negative language can help build rapport and trust with the other person.

Thirdly, be clear and concise. Navy SEALs are known for their ability to communicate effectively in high-pressure situations. To adopt this ethos, it's essential to be clear and concise in your communication. This means being direct and getting to the point without beating around the bush.

Fourthly, show empathy. Another essential aspect of effective communication is showing empathy. This means understanding and acknowledging the other person's feelings and emotions. It helps build trust and rapport with the other person.

Fifthly, practice active listening. Active listening is a key component of effective communication. It involves paying attention to what the other person is saying, asking clarifying questions, and providing feedback. By practicing active listening, you can improve your ability to understand and respond to the other person's needs and concerns.

Finally, be adaptable. One of the core principles of NLP is that communication is always a two-way street. Therefore, it's important to be adaptable and flexible in your communication style, adapting to the other person's communication style and preferences. In addition, continuously improve your communication skills by seeking feedback and studying new techniques.

Life Energy Wheel

The eight sections in the life energy wheel represent balance. Rank your level of satisfaction with each life area by drawing a curved line to create a new outer edge. The new perimeter of the circle represents the Wheel of life. How bumpy would the ride be if this were an actual wheel? The areas of the life energy wheel typically include Physical, Emotional, Mental, Spiritual, Financial, Career, and Social. But remember, these are just examples, and your priorities and values may vary.

The Life Energy Wheel is a tool used to assess and balance various aspects of our lives. It is based on the idea that our lives are interconnected and that each area affects the others. Here's how to use the Life Energy Wheel:

Step 1: Draw or print a copy of the Life Energy Wheel. The Wheel is divided into different sections, each representing another aspect of our lives. These sections include:

• Physical Health: This includes things like diet, exercise, and sleep.

• Emotional Health: This includes our feelings and emotions, such as happiness, sadness, anger, and anxiety.

• Mental Health: This includes our thoughts and beliefs, such as our values, attitudes, and opinions.

• Spiritual Health: This includes our sense of purpose, meaning, and connection to something greater than ourselves.

• Relationships: This includes our connections with others, such as family, friends, and romantic partners.
• Finances: This includes our money and financial well-being.

• Career: This includes our work and professional goals.

• Fun and Recreation: This includes hobbies, leisure activities, and things we enjoy doing.

Step 2: Assess each area of the Wheel. Rate each area from 1-4, with 1 being the lowest and 4 being the highest. Be honest with yourself and think about how satisfied you are with each area of your life.

Step 3: Connect the dots. Draw lines connecting the ratings you gave for each section. This will create a visual representation of your Life Energy Wheel. The goal is to create a smooth, balanced wheel with no low areas.

Step 4: Identify areas that need improvement. Take a look at your Life Energy Wheel and identify areas that are low. These are areas that you may want to focus on improving.

Step 5: Take action. Develop a plan for how you can improve the areas of your Life Energy Wheel that are low. This may involve setting goals, seeking support from others, or making changes to your lifestyle.

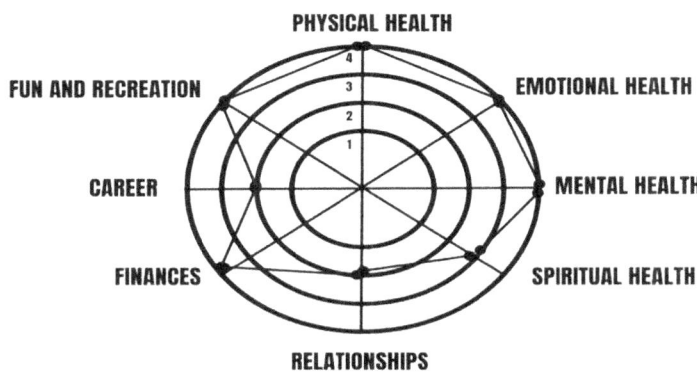

Regularly assessing and balancing your Life Energy Wheel can create a more satisfying and fulfilling life that aligns with your values and goals.

About the Author

Frederick is a seasoned expert in the field of high-performance optimization, equipped with a wealth of experience and knowledge. With his guidance, he can help lead you on a transformative journey from an underdog to a champion. Frederick will teach you the ways of the inner warrior mindset, helping you eliminate limiting beliefs that may be hindering your success.

Throughout his life, Frederick has been an athlete for over four decades, competing in various sports, including baseball, basketball, football, tennis, powerlifting, weightlifting, body-building, and track. In college, he was a track sprinter at the division one level. His dream of representing the United States in international competitions began after watching the Olympics, and he went on to achieve that dream, representing the U.S. at world cup competitions and the Pan-Americans in the sport of Olympic Weightlifting.

Despite not being the tallest, biggest, fastest, strongest, or smartest athlete and student, Frederick approached every day as an opportunity to improve and learn from his mistakes. He motivates and inspires others to embrace their inner underdog as fuel to become a champion in all areas of life. Frederick is certified in Neuro-Linguistic Programming, high-performance coaching, and sports performance hypnosis, a USA Weightlifting Sports Performance Coach, and a six-sigma green belt certified. He holds a degree in electrical engineering and is the author of "Financial Game Plan for Your Dollars and Cents: A Step-by-step, common-sense Approach to Making the Right Financial Decisions" and co-author of the international bestseller "1% More: The hidden force to creating extraordinary results in life & business." Fred is one of the co-founders and co-host of the Extraordinary Being Movement.

AUTHOR CONTACT INFORMATION
Frederick Martinez, Optimal High Performance Strategist
Website: fredmartinez.info
Website: wtfredbook.com
Facebook: https://www.facebook.com/whatthefredbook
Instagram: https://www.instagram.com/wtfredbook/

www.ingramcontent.com/pod-product-compliance
Lightning Source LLC
Chambersburg PA
CBHW071400120626

46546CB00002B/759